THE SUNDERLAND STORY

AN ILLUSTRATED FOOTBALL HISTORY

ROB MASON

Dedicated to Jean, Bob, Gordon and Barbara Mason.

A Pillar Box Red Publication

© 1999
Published by Pillar Box Red Publishing Ltd., Edinburgh.

Printed in the EU.

ISBN: 1-84204-008-1

Researched and written by Rob Mason.

Photographs supplied by EMPICS, The North East Press & from the author's personal collection. We have been unable to trace the sources of all of the author's pictures, but any photographer involved is invited to contact the publishers in writing providing proof of copyright.

This completely independent publication has been prepared without any involvement on the part of Sunderland Football Club or the Premiership and has no connection whatsoever with either organisation.

Whilst every effort has been made to ensure the accuracy of information contained within this book, the publishers cannot be held responsible for any errors or omissions.

Views expressed are those of the author and do not necessarily represent those of the publishers.

CONTENTS

FOREWORD

Sunderland have always been my club. Having grown up supporting them, it was an unbelievable thrill to get the chance to actually play for 'The Lads'. In every one of my two hundred and ninety games, I was fulfilling a dream.

I would have loved to have played more games and years for Sunderland but it was not to be. At the 1985 League Cup Final, when injury ruled me out of Norwich's team to play Sunderland, I was given the cup by Mick Channon so I could take it over to the Sunderland supporters, who were showing their class by choking back their disappointment and applauding Norwich, who had won 1-0. I had to choke back my own tears as they chanted my name over and over. It was the best moment of my career and I hadn't even been playing.

The Roker Roar was as famous as the club and rightly so. There was never a divide between the players and the supporters. We were all chasing the same goal and that is still the case, as 1999 captain, Kevin Ball, has made clear.

Sunderland supporters have always been very special. They don't just support their team on a matchday; they love it every day and are the most knowledgeable of fans. Throughout the club's history, the team have had some great years and some lean ones but the support has always been different class. Even when down to the true hardcore in the bad times, the players have always been able to count on the kind of backing that has never existed at most clubs.

Everyone on Wearside regards Sunderland as a very big club. Historically they have been, of course, with Championship and cup-winning sides of great players like Raich Carter, Len Shackleton and Jimmy Montgomery. Now that the Stadium of Light demonstrates Sunderland's ambition, I, like every Sunderland supporter, hope to see Championship and cup-winning teams in the future as well as from the glorious past.

Gary Rowell

GARY ROWELL

Seaham born Gary Rowell is Sunderland's record post-war goalscorer, with 102 goals. Top scorer in six seasons between 1978 and 1984, with only injury preventing him from scoring even more, Rowell was the clinical close-range finisher who had the knack of being in the right place at the right time and possessed the composure to make sure he scored when the opportunity was there.

Probably the club's best ever penalty taker, with only Jackie Mordue either side of World War One and Billy Clunas from the twenties as serious rivals for the title, Rowell included a spot kick in his never-to-be-forgotten hat-trick against Newcastle in a 4-1 win at St. James' Park in 1979.

INTRODUCTION

Sunderland are once again a club that people are taking notice of! Playing in the best stadium in England, regularly attracting crowds of over forty thousand in the First Division in 1999, achieving a record total of 105 points to stride into the Premiership, then selling all 36,000 season tickets available was bound to make people nationwide start to see Sunderland as a major club. Sunderland supporters though have always believed that Sunderland are *not* a big club - they know that they're potentially one of the biggest! Only Man Utd and Liverpool recorded higher average gates than the Wearsiders in 1998-99 and when even Sunderland's reserve side can attract crowds in excess of 33,000 then it is obvious that one of the previously deepest sleeping giants of English football has woken up and is beginning to stretch itself.

The Roker Roar was famed for its volume and passion in Roker Park's ninety-nine year history and now that Sunderland are established at the Sunderland Stadium of Light, there is the distinct possibility that a bright new chapter in the club's history is just beginning. The fact that Sunderland have sought and received permission to extend their capacity to 48,000 and have the potential to extend the ground to a total of 63,000 provides a further indication of the ambition of the club. Should England be awarded the World Cup in 2006, the Stadium of Light has already been designated a Class 'A' ground and indeed has already received recognition in the form of the FA choosing to play England's October 1999 friendly with Belgium there when Wembley is unavailable.

Having won six Championships before the Second World War and survived in the Football League from 1890 until 1958 without ever being relegated, Sunderland cherished their claim to be the only club never to play outside the top flight. However, since that first ever relegation in 1958, 'The Lads' have become one of the proverbial 'Yo-Yo' clubs and haven't finished in the top half of the top division since ninth place was achieved in 1956.

Considering this prolonged period of failure at the top level - with the sole exception of the glorious day in 1973 when Sunderland became the first Second Division side in forty-two years to win the FA Cup - it is amazing that Sunderland can still count on such sizeable and optimistic support. Then again, it is the fact that Sunderland have such fanatical followers that makes them such a fascinating club.

WE GET KNOCKED DOWN,
BUT WE GET UP AGAIN
(1998 & 1999)

"There's only one Michael Gray", reverberated around Wembley Stadium seconds after Sunderland-born Gray had seen Charlton goalkeeper, Sasa Ilic, save his decisive penalty in the 1998 Play-Off Final.

The celebrations of the Londoners were drowned out by the throaty roars of Wearside fans, who choked back yet another crushing disappointment at the 'Venue of Letdowns' to empathise with one of their own. Gray had been one of the stalwarts of an exciting Sunderland side that had gone so close to automatic promotion after such a terrible start. Manager Peter Reid's head had been called for after a 4-0 hammering at Reading, ten games into the season, that left Sunderland in twelfth place.

Showing spirit as well as skill, Sunderland had scorched their way up the table to finish in third place with 90 points - a record number to miss promotion with, just twelve months after a record 40 points had proved insufficient to stave off relegation. Champions, Forest, had been played off their own patch as Sunderland demolished them 3-0 but the head start given at the outset of the campaign proved insurmountable and so the Red 'n' White Army headed for Wembley, where Sunderland had lost on their last four appearances (including the 1988 League Centenary appearance against Wigan) without mustering a single goal. This time, though, they would play in one of the finest games ever witnessed beneath the twin towers, find the net four times and then score six successive spot kicks, still without it being enough to bring success.

Starting the following season after such a gut-wrenching occasion, it would have been understandable if the side had struggled in the way defeated Play-Off Final teams often do. It was half expected in the light of the carry-over effect experienced twelve months earlier, when, despite all the talk of bouncing back after relegation, the side started, not like an express train but like a reject from the Thomas the Tank Engine collection backing up a country siding.

This time, though, there would be no hitting the buffers. Sunderland swept all before them.

Michael Gray

Not even losing record signing, Lee Clark, with a broken leg in the first half of the first game, or losing prolific goalscorer, Kevin Phillips, for four months after he'd scored in eight of the opening ten matches, could derail Sunderland. Unbeaten until the twenty-fifth match, not one of the club's four sides lost at any level until the final day in September.

The strength of the squad Peter Reid had assembled proved to be Sunderland's might. When the reserve side clinched the Pontins Premier League ahead of Man Utd and Liverpool just a year after winning promotion to the league, it highlighted how far Sunderland had come as a club. The first team were out of sight at the top of the First Division, finishing eighteen points ahead of runners-up, Bradford City, whom they had beaten away from home despite putting centre forward, Niall Quinn, in goal after goalkeeper, Thomas Sorensen, was carried off!

In 1998-99 the side created records quicker than The Beatles! No team in any division had ever managed 105 points; only three defeats was the lowest ever for a forty-six game league campaign; 29 clean sheets in all competitions was a club record; only 18 goals were conceded at home, representing the best club performance since the 34-game season of 1901, while at the other end of the pitch, 'the Lads' were the country's leading scorers for the second year running and Kevin Phillips became the second-fastest Sunderland player to reach fifty goals for the club since the war.

No-one had done more for SAFC than captain, Kevin Ball and there was no prouder man than 'Bally' when he lifted the Championship trophy after Sunderland had come from behind to beat fourth-placed Birmingham City to ensure that Sunderland had beaten every other team in the division during their triumphant campaign.

The lap of honour was fantastically emotional. The frustration that had been bottled up inside the players, fans and everyone associated with the club, was simultaneously released into a prolonged outburst of pure joy. The Stadium of Light sound system is famous for blasting out Prokofiev's, 'Dance of the Knights' and Republica's, 'Ready to Go' as the teams run out but on this occasion it was songs like Van Morrison's, 'Days like These' and the promotion anthem, 'We're On Our Way' that added to the occasion. As Michael Gray approached the towering West Stand, Chumbawumba's, 'Tubthumping' sounded out and seemed especially poignant. The supporters of the likes of Man Utd, Arsenal and Liverpool will never understand what it means to a

Sunderland supporter to be top of the league.

To experience the highest highs, you have to have experienced the lowest lows. Sunderland have spent forty years in a wilderness away from the top half of the top flight. For a club of the stature Sunderland once enjoyed to sink to the Third Division, as they did in 1987, was a catastrophe of Dickensian proportions. For any Sunderland supporter less than half a century old, really they have overwhelmingly had to endure the worst of times and now, at last, there is optimism that the new millennium will usher in the best of times, as Sunderland seek to re-join the elite.

ORIGINS
(1879-1886)

Once the club had got over the difficult years involved in establishing an organisation that would have the ability to survive financially, Sunderland experienced the best of times very quickly. The first club to be elected to the two-year-old Football League in 1890, the Wearsiders quickly dominated it.

Seventh in their first season, when the deduction of two points cost them fifth place, Sunderland, having found their feet in the competition, went on to win it three times in the next four years, being runners-up in the year they were pipped for the title. Dubbed, 'The Team of All the Talents', by William McGregor, the founder of the Football League, after he watched them destroy Aston Villa 7-2 at Villa's Perry Barr ground on April 5th, 1890, Sunderland dominated the sport.

In 1892-93, when they retained the title, Sunderland became the first side to record 100 goals in a season - even though there were only thirty matches! That was the first year of a two-division English league, so Sunderland became the first winners of the First Division, having been the last winners of the single division Football League.

In those days, the stars of the side were Scottish international goalkeeper, Teddy Doig, forward, Johnny Campbell and captain, Hugh Wilson, although 'the Team of All the Talents' evidently didn't have a weak link.

Teddy Doig won four Championship medals with Sunderland and was known as 'the Prince of Goalkeepers.' Johnny Campbell took only 53 games to score 50 goals and was top scorer in five of Sunderland's first six league campaigns. In 1891-92 Sunderland scored an amazing 217 goals in all games, including the many friendlies played and Campbell was reckoned to have scored at least half of them! A well-built speed merchant, Campbell was the First Division's top scorer three times. Wilson was the only player to play in both Sunderland's first league game in 1890 and the first match at Roker Park eight years later. A Scottish international, he was renowned for his long, one-handed throw-in, which prompted the powers-that-be to change the rules of the game so that two hands had to be used to throw the ball in. A most influential captain, in 1896 he also became the first ever Sunderland player to be sent off and was the first Sunderland player to score a penalty in the league.

While Sunderland were a leading power in the game in the final decade of the nineteenth century, they weren't involved in the opening of the Football League. When the League was formed, it was dominated by clubs from the north west and midlands. Sunderland was felt to be too far north and so, initially, Sunderland weren't able to become Founder Members. Sunderland had been in existence for nine years when the Football League kicked off in 1888.

The club was formed in October 1879 as Sunderland and District Teachers' Association Football Club by James Allan, a former Edinburgh schoolmaster who came to work at Hendon, in Sunderland, at Thomas Street Boys' School. Allan organised a meeting in The British Day School on the corner of Norfolk Street and Borough Road. The building is still there and is now a hotel. Allan must take the credit for introducing football to Sunderland and at the inaugural meeting he took the post of vice-captain, with John Singleton elected captain and another teacher, John Graystone, taking on the role of secretary.

The Norfolk Hotel, Sunderland. The Club was founded here in 1879.

Initially based south of the River Wear, the club's first ground was at the Blue House Field in Hendon, a site now occupied by Valley Road Infants School, while the club's first headquarters were in the now demolished Norman Street.

Site of the first ground from across Robinson Terrace Cricket Ground.
New Valley Road Infants School.

Sunderland's first competitive match was played at the Blue House Field over a year later, on November 13th 1880, when Ferryhill beat the Wearsiders 1-0. James Allan and goalkeeper, John Singleton, both played in the following line up: Singleton, Taylor, Shirlaw, Gibbons, Anderson, Watson, Barron, Dove, Woodward, Chappell and Allan. Allan was a forward and he scored twice in Sunderland's next match, along with Watson and Elliott, as a first ever victory was registered against Ovingham at the Blue House Field a fortnight later. A 1-1 home draw with Burnopfield then preceded a first ever away game on December 18th 1880, at Rowlands Gill, where Burnopfield were beaten 2-0, with Allan scoring both of the goals.

Two more games are recorded from that season, a 5-0 drubbing against The Rangers of Newcastle in the semi final of the Northumberland and Durham Challenge Cup (which had been reached by the win against Burnopfield) and a goalless draw in a return at Ferryhill. The Rangers of Newcastle had nothing to do with the clubs that grew to be Newcastle United but as they played at St James' Park, in Newcastle, it is interesting to note that Sunderland played at St James' before the 'Magpies' did.

Sunderland stayed at the Blue House Field for one more season but the annual rent of £10 was proving difficult to manage and so the decision was taken to allow non - teachers to join the club. The 'and District Teachers' Association' was dropped from the club name of Sunderland and Alderman J. Potts became the first President. It is believed that the club briefly used a pitch near The Cedars, just up the road from the Blue House Field, before the end of the season.

Briefly the site of a little-known home ground between The Cedars and Percy Terrace, 1881.

It was appropriate that Sunderland started at the Blue House Field, as in those early days they wore blue rather than the red and white stripes for which the club is famous. Blue shirts and knickerbockers, with a white stripe on the knickerbockers, were the order of the day in an age when players also wore a tassled cap! On the pitch, the club enjoyed mixed fortunes as they met nine different teams including 'North Eastern', whom they played three times.

The start of the 1882-83 season saw Sunderland move to Groves Field in the Ashbrooke area of the town but before the end of the decade, the Blue House Field would feature again in Wearside football's history, when the rival Sunderland Albion Club based itself there. Sunderland's stay in Ashbrooke was brief, just a few months and four home games, in fact, before they made a significant move to the north of the River Wear, where they have remained ever since.

One of the quartet of games played at Groves Field saw Sunderland exceed their officially recorded record score of 11-1 (v Fairfield, FA Cup 1st rd, 1895), when Stanley Star were defeated 12-1 in the first round of the Northumberland and Durham

Groves Field, Ashbrooke, the last of the grounds south of the river.

Challenge Cup in January 1883. Sunderland got to the final, where they went down to Tyne, 2-0, at Brandling Park in Newcastle, in what proved to be Sunderland's only appearance in the competition's final, as after that they competed in the Durham Challenge Cup after the County Associations split because of the cost of travelling.

The move across the River Wear came in time for the start of the 1883-84 season, when the club moved to Roker, with which it would later become inextricably linked because of its near-century-long residence at Roker Park. However, this move was to Horatio Street, to a ground that was often known as 'The Dolly Field.' It also ran alongside Cooper Street and the ground is sometimes called that, too, in the same way that Loftus Road, South Africa Road and Rangers Stadium vie for the title of QPR's current ground. The pitch is long gone and like Roker Park, it became houses. Appleby Terrace and Givens Street now cover the site but you can still go for a drink in 'The Wolseley', which the players used as a changing room in those days.

Sunderland did well at their new home, beating Castle Eden 8-1 in their first match there and by the end of the season had won their first trophy - the Durham Challenge Cup. The win wasn't without its problems, though. Firstly, there was no cup to receive, as the Durham FA didn't have the funds to buy one for its first tournament; and secondly, the final had to be replayed following complaints about the behaviour of Sunderland's supporters.

Darlington provided the opposition in the final, which was the first game where an indication of the size of the crowd watching Sunderland is recorded. Between one and two thousand people are estimated to have been at the first final which took place at the Newcastle Road Cricket Ground. Although Sunderland won 4-3 in a match refereed by Durham FA Chairman, Mr Alfred Grundy of Whitburn, the game had to be replayed at Birtley, with the President of the FA - Major Francis Marindin, RE - in charge. Marindin was the founder of the Royal Engineers and refereed no less than nine FA Cup Finals. Goals from McDonald and Joyce ensured a 2-0 replay win and eight months later Sunderland captain, James McMillan, finally received the trophy, which had been bought with proceeds of the inaugural tournament. The original final referee, Mr. Grundy, presented it.

By the time McMillan received the trophy, Sunderland had moved grounds again and had entered the FA Cup for the first time. Abbs Field, in Fulwell, was the new home.

Situated on the site that for many years later was the Central Laundry, just a couple of decent goal kicks from the Fulwell End at Roker Park, Abbs Field had the advantage of being walled in and so, for the first time, the club could prosper by taking gate money instead of a collection, with 3d (1.25p) being the charge.

The opening match at Abbs Field took place in late September 1884, when Birtley were beaten 2-0. Home wins of 8-2 and 5-1 were achieved before Sunderland's first ever FA Cup tie took them to Redcar on November 8th. Beaten 3-1 by goals from Bulman, Harrison and Agar for the home side, Sunderland's scorer was right winger, Don McColl, who two months later tried his hand in goal at home to Port Glasgow. As the Scots won 11-1 it was just as well he quickly returned to outfield duties.

Site of Abbs Field.

Once again Sunderland and Darlington met in the final of the Durham Challenge Cup but this time it was Darlington's turn to triumph. Sunderland protested about their 3-0 defeat at Feethams and refused to enter the competition the following year, when the Durham FA didn't look on their complaint as sympathetically as they had on that of 'The Quakers' a year earlier.

1885-86 saw Sunderland begin to wear red and white rather than blue but the shirts were red and white halves in the Blackburn style rather than stripes. White knickerbockers and red and white socks completed the kit. Once again Sunderland went out of the FA Cup at Redcar in the 1st Qualifying Round but interest was retained by increased games against sides from further afield than the north east and indeed, Sunderland began to travel more widely. On February 27th 1886, 'The Lads' played outside of England for the first time, beating Hearts 2-1 in Edinburgh, with founder and former Edinburgh schoolmaster, James Allan, in the line up.

Crowds at Abbs Field had increased to as high as three and a half thousand and so, in 1886, Sunderland were on the move once more. The rent at Abbs Field had risen from £2.10s (£2.50) in the first season to £15 in the second and last; and indeed, the move to Newcastle Road was made before the end of the season.

Site of the Newcastle Road Ground. Home of the 'Team of All The Talents', 1890s, five minutes walk from the Stadium of Light.

'THE TEAM OF ALL THE TALENTS' & SUNDERLAND'S OTHER TEAM (1886-1898).

Newcastle Road was the scene of phenomenal success. League football in Sunderland began there and soon 'The Team of All the Talents' established Sunderland as a giant of the game, with three league titles in four years. Sunderland's home from March 13th 1886, the Newcastle Road ground had staged the 1884 Durham FA Challenge Cup Final just under two years earlier. That Sunderland · Darlington fixture was repeated when the same sides met in the first match after Sunderland's move there. A crowd of one thousand saw goals from Jobes, Smith and Hunter give Sunderland a 3-1 win and a week later, James Allan got a hat trick in a 3-3 home draw with Birtley.

The first full season at Newcastle Road (1886 · 87) was the first time Sunderland wore red and white stripes. It also brought Sunderland's first home game in the FA Cup (or 'English Cup' as it was then known) when Morpeth Harriers were soundly beaten, 7-2, in a preliminary round, before extra time was needed to see off Newcastle West End in the first qualifying round. However, although Newcastle West End were beaten 2-1, as with the 1884 Durham Cup Final win over Darlington, Sunderland were ordered to replay – this time after the Tynesiders complained about the game being played in bad light and 'The Lads' were subsequently eliminated 1-0. This was the first FA Cup tie ever played by either of the clubs who eventually amalgamated to form Newcastle United.

There was cup success in the first full season at Newcastle Road, though, when Darlington were defeated again in the Durham Challenge Cup and the ground hosted three visiting Scottish sides in the first week of 1887, including Glasgow Rangers, who were beaten 1-0 on New Year's Day.

A record crowd of 8,000, still paying 3d each, attended Newcastle Road the following season in an early indication of cup fever on Wearside. FA Cup progress had been made against Morpeth Harriers · in a game that was once more replayed after a protest · and Newcastle West End, before a 2-2 draw away to Middlesbrough. The replay crowd knew that a bye into the last sixteen awaited the winners of what was still a qualifying game and roared Sunderland to a 4-2 win after trailing 2-0 at half time.

In those days a good lawyer must have been as important as a good centre forward, because yet again the match became a cause for dispute. Unhappy that three Scotsmen in the Sunderland line up, Monaghan, Hastings and Richardson, played as professionals, the Teessiders complained and as a result, Sunderland were disqualified and the players suspended for three months. 'Boro went on to the quarter finals but never got further than that until 1997.

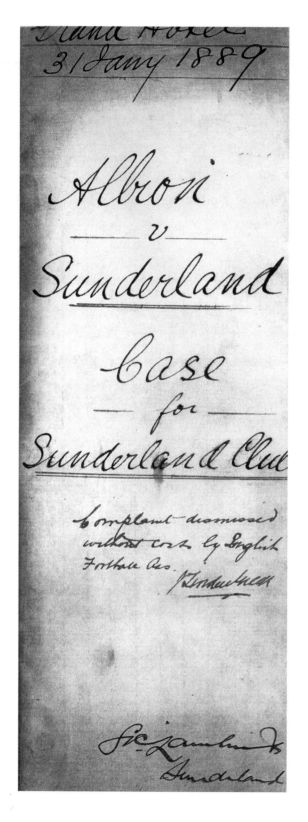

SUNDERLAND ALBION

The controversy over the disqualification of the Sunderland players had major implications. Two months after the judgement of the full inquiry over the affair in London, original club founder, James Allan, held a meeting on March 13th 1888 at The Empress Hotel in Sunderland to form a breakaway club, Sunderland Albion.

Several of Sunderland's Scottish players including the trio at the centre of the storm, went with Allan, whose new club returned to Sunderland's original home at The Blue House Field. May 5th is a significant date in the minds of all Sunderland supporters, as it is the anniversary of one of the club's greatest days, when Leeds were beaten in the 1973 FA Cup Final and it was on this day in 1888 that Sunderland Albion played their first match. Allan's Albion beat Shankhouse 3-0 and followed up their success with a 3-1 win over Newcastle West End. Albion existed for four years and were to be a thorn in Sunderland's side.

Before the split at Sunderland, a record defeat, 11-0 at home to the Scots of Cambuslang the day after New Year's Day, didn't disturb the progress of the club. Increased revenue allowed the ground to be built up and headquarters to be extended, although a loss of £370 was shown for the season. However, there was more success on the pitch with another Durham Challenge Cup win, Bishop Auckland Church Institute being beaten in the final at Darlington.

1888 - 89 was to be a make-or-break season for the two Sunderland clubs, who engaged in a Victorian, 'this town ain't big enough for both of us', showdown. Albion were a substantial enough organisation to field four sides. Heavily Scots dominated, they used The Waverley Hotel in Hendon as their HQ.

When the two Sunderland clubs were paired together in the 4th qualifying round of the FA Cup, Sunderland withdrew from the competition. It was claimed that the reason was that cups had proved their worth in establishing football but it was generally believed that the real reason was that Sunderland didn't want Albion to benefit from the huge financial boost such a derby match would provide. Albion duly took their place in the first round, where Stewart was their scorer in a 3-1 defeat at Grimsby Town.

Under local pressure to play Albion, especially after also withdrawing from the Durham Challenge Cup when paired with them, Sunderland offered to play if the proceeds went to charity. Albion held out for a game where they would take their share of the receipts and eventually Sunderland had little option but to relent.

James Allan wrote to Sunderland on the day before the match asking if Albion members would be admitted free and requesting details of how money would be collected and where the gate money would be counted, as the atmosphere of distrust heightened.

A crowd variously claimed to be between ten and eighteen thousand packed into Newcastle Road on December 1st 1888 to see a game as keenly anticipated as a modern day derby with Newcastle. Albion were unbeaten in thirteen games (they were yet to meet Grimsby) but Sunderland, who had been strengthened by several new arrivals since the split, won 2-0. As with many heavyweight boxing contests, a rematch was immediately sought. When Sunderland eventually agreed, they wouldn't entertain thoughts of playing at The Blue House Field and so Newcastle Road was again the venue when the sides met six weeks after the original meeting.

In a bitterly contested match, Albion gained a 2-0 lead by half time, only for Sunderland to fight back and eventually score a most controversial winner three minutes from time. This was before nets were used and Albion were certain that Breconridge's winner had gone over the bar, or 'crosspiece.' All hell broke loose! Albion's players stormed off when the goal was given and as they left, they were heavily stoned and Allan - who had been Albion's Umpire, or linesman/assistant referee, in the game – had his eye injured so badly he had to have surgery.

Albion protested to the FA, secretary Thomas Jobling stating that, "I beg to lodge a formal complaint as to the brutal conduct of the Sunderland supporters on January 12th in the match Sunderland v Albion. Our players were openly threatened in the field, as was also our umpire and during the latter period of the game, mud was thrown at our players and umpire. Mr Stacey, the referee, was hooted and howled at by the crowd at any decision he gave in favour of the Albion and after the match, the brake conveying our players from the field was stoned and several of our players, including our umpire, injured. I am only giving you the head of our objection but can support further details by witnesses if necessary."

A Committee of Inquiry was set up by the Durham FA, to whom the FA referred the matter and this met at The Grand Hotel on January 31st, when Albion's case was dismissed.

Albion had also written to the Sheffield referee, Mr W.H. Stacey, who replied, "I am much surprised and hurt at the contents of your letter....I had nothing to regret and the only regrettable part was the Albion men leaving the field before time..."

Meanwhile, within three days of the match, Albion were asking Sunderland for a third game: Jobling wrote, "The Albion Committee consider that the disadvantages that they have played under have prevented them from showing their true form in their two matches with Sunderland. They are of the opinion that it would take a very superior team, indeed, to beat Sunderland on their own ground under the conditions that the Albion have experienced. They, however, have such faith in the ability of their present team to beat the Sunderland present team upon level terms that they are willing to play them a match on a neutral ground (Darlington, Newcastle, Middlesbrough or Stockton) or at Hendon. The winners to receive a silver cup, value £20, which has been generously offered by an independent gentleman. An early answer will oblige. I have sent this to the papers."

Sunderland, though, had now played and beaten Albion twice and had no desire to do so again. It was three years until they were to meet again. By the 1892 Easter Monday encounter, Sunderland were not only in the Football League but were its champions and Albion were thrashed 6-1. A few weeks later, Sunderland finally played Albion at their Blue House Ground but by then Albion were sliding into oblivion and only 2,000 thought it worth turning up to see Sunderland beat them 8-0. Albion, who had won the Durham Challenge Cup in their first season and had continued to play regularly in the FA Cup, finally folded in August 1892.

That 1888-89 tussle for supremacy between the Wearside clubs was fought while the Football League played its first season. The "Invincibles" of Preston North End were unbeaten in doing the double but came to Sunderland at the end of April and were soundly beaten, 4-1, before a big crowd of around 10,000. Despite this, Sunderland's application to join the league saw them collect a mere two votes.

During the summer of 1889 there was a massive turnover of players at Sunderland. Chairman, James Marr, President, Robert Thompson, Treasurer ,Samuel Tyzack (a coal owner, who had taken over from Allan) and John Graystone, who had remained at

Letter from Thomas Jobling.

"Albion" Football Club,
SUNDERLAND.

18 Whitehall Terrace,
Hylton Road,
Jany 15 1889

Dear Sir

The Albion Committee consider that the dis-advantages that they have played under have prevented them from showing their true form in their two matches with Sunderland.

They are of opinion that it would take a very superior team indeed to beat Sunderland on their own ground under the conditions that the Albion have experienced these two matches.

They, however, have such faith in the ability of their present team to beat the Sunderland present team upon level terms that they are willing to play them a match, either 3 weeks on neutral ground (Darlington, Newcastle, Middlesbro or Stockton) or at Hendon, the winners to receive a silver cup value £20 which has been generously offered by an independent gentleman.

An early answer will

24

"Albion" Football Club,

SUNDERLAND.

3, Whitehall Terrace,

Hylton Road,

Nov. 30th 1888

Mr W. T. Wallace

Dear Sir,

I will feel obliged if you will inform me if the members of the Albion will be admitted free on production of membership card.

What time the gates will be opened. What system you have of taking gate If by sale of tickets, Are the tickets collected? Where you intend to count gate. I leave the other matters in your hands.

Yours truly

James Allan

Letter from James Allan.

25

Sunderland from the earliest days, rebuilt the club and took it into a new dimension.

Several of Scotland's best players were signed, including three from 1888 Scottish Cup winners, Renton, who had previously visited Sunderland. One of these was Johnny Campbell, who played in Renton's April 1888 win on Wearside and would go on to be one of the club's greatest ever goalscorers. It was the birth of 'The Team of All The Talents' - the most successful team in Sunderland's history.

A fourth Durham Challenge Cup was won (Darlington again being the runners up) and the FA Cup first round proper was reached for the first time - Blackburn Rovers winning 4-2 in extra time of a first game at Blackburn to put them on the road to winning the cup. Without doubt, though, the most important game of the season was played on April 5th 1890. On that day, Sunderland visited Aston Villa and trounced them 7-2, causing the founder of the Football League, William McGregor, to describe them as, 'The Team of All The Talents.' Come the end of the season, the AGM of the Football League was held on May 2nd at The Douglas Hotel in Manchester and Sunderland were elected as the first team to be admitted to the league after the founder members.

Sunderland replaced Stoke City to become the first league club north of Burnley, having promised to help visiting sides with their travelling expenses so far north. The club pointed out that they'd be making eleven long journeys compared to the single long journey teams would make to visit Wearside. Chairman Marr and Reverend Hindle of Eppleton, an ex-player who represented Sunderland, also reminded league members that most of them had already visited Sunderland for lucrative friendlies.

Showing the sort of ambition needed for success, Sunderland had a policy of signing top class young players and almost invariably these were from north of the border. Two important newcomers for the first league season were Hugh Wilson and James Millar. Wilson would captain the team in their glory years, while Millar became one of only two men to win four Championship medals with the club.

Champions, Preston, were beaten 6-3 in a pre season friendly to whet the appetite for league football, which commenced on Wearside on September 13th 1890, when Burnley surprised everyone by winning 3-2.

Spence scored both of Sunderland's goals in their first ever league game, although Burnley ran out 3-2 victors. Burnley were the only one of their league opponents they hadn't previously played. The Sunderland line up was: Kirtley, Porteous, Oliver, Wilson, Auld, Gibson, Spence, Millar, Campbell, Scott and D. Hannah.

A midweek home defeat against Wolves, after Sunderland led 3-0, resulted in the immediate signing of goalkeeper, Teddy Doig, who was to match Millar's eventual record of four Championship medals with Sunderland. He made an immediate difference, keeping a clean sheet as Sunderland won their first away match 4-0 at West Bromwich Albion, only to be fined and docked the points because Doig hadn't been correctly registered!

Johnny Campbell scored Sunderland's first hat-trick in a 5-2 away win at Bolton Wanderers on October 25th 1890. The following January, Jimmy Millar scored the first home hat trick in a 4-0 triumph over Notts County.

With Newcastle-born Tom Watson · who had established Newcastle West End and played a leading role in helping Newcastle East End · in charge, after being approached by John Graystone, Sunderland went from strength to strength and were beaten only once at home in six years following Doig's signing. Seventh in their first season as a league side, Sunderland, nonetheless, showed what was in store by reaching their first FA Cup semi final, going down to Notts County in a replay at Bramall Lane.

A year later, Bramall Lane was again the scene of FA Cup semi-final defeat for Sunderland (against Aston Villa) but they took the Championship by five points from runners-up Preston, scoring five, six or seven goals in seven of their twenty-six games. A 100% home record can never be beaten, while a run of thirteen successive wins has never been matched since. Doig and fullback, Tom Porteous, were ever-presents.

Johnny Campbell top-scored in the first Championship season, with 28 goals in 25 games, while Hannah (16), Millar (16) and Smith (10) also reached double figures.

Tom Porteous became the first player to be capped while with Sunderland. He played in a 4-1 win for England over Wales at Sunderland's Newcastle Road ground on March 7th 1891. A crowd of 15,000 watched the British Championship match. Sunderland's many top-class Scottish players at the time missed out on caps because of the Scottish policy of not playing Anglo-Scots.

1892-93 was the first year of the two-division Football League and it saw Sunderland dominate the opposition every bit as much as they did in 1998-99's record 105-point campaign. Campbell again led the scoring stakes, with 30 goals from the maximum 30 league games, as Sunderland became the first club to score 100 league goals in a season, a feat not beaten until the league programme was extended to 42 games after the First World War. Runners-up, Preston, were a massive eleven points behind in those two- points-for-a-win days.

In 1892-93, Sunderland scored an amazing 42 away goals in only 15 games. This remains a club record, with only the 41 goals in the 46-game (23 away) lower division campaigns of 1987-88 and 1998-99 coming near to beating it.

It's a measure of how dominant Sunderland were in the League's formative years that the 1893-94 season was a disappointment, when only a runners-up spot could be managed but normal service was resumed the following year, when the Championship was won for the third time in four seasons. No wonder they were called, "The Team of All the Talents." That was the club's last Championship win of the nineteenth century and the last major trophy for the side that established Sunderland as one of the game's giants.

Derbyshire side, Fairfield, were the victims of Sunderland's record score of 11-1 in league or cup, when they were walloped in the FA Cup in February 1895, with Jimmy

Millar becoming the first of four players in the history of Sunderland to score five in a match and former Sunderland Albion player, Jimmy Hannah, weighing in with a hat-trick of his own. Derbyshire sides must have been in awe of trips to Sunderland. On the first day of the season, Derby County had also conceded eleven on Wearside. However, in their case, after trailing 3-0 at half time with a reserve referee in charge, the real match official arrived late and re-started the match at 0-0. A second chance for Derby made no difference to the outcome, though, as Sunderland strode to an 8-0 victory. What great days to support 'The Lads'!

Of course, all great things come to an end and 1895-96 saw the team's fortunes begin to fade. Fifth place was the first time Sunderland had been out of the top two since their first league campaign. Only one more goal was scored in total than had been managed in home games alone a year earlier and in the close season, manager, Tom Watson, departed for Liverpool. Eight years later, Watson persuaded legendary goalkeeper, Teddy Doig, to follow him to Merseyside. The pair are now buried within twenty feet of each other in Liverpool.

Watson's departure followed boardroom changes which revolved around the club being wound up in July 1896 in order to become a limited liability company. As part of the transformation James Potts Henderson took over as chairman and very like Bob Murray a century later he was to prove the catalyst for the club moving into a new stadium for a new century.

'The Team of All the Talents' won the League Championship three times in four seasons between 1892 and 1895 and reached the FA Cup semi final three times in the same period.

New manager/secretary, Robert Campbell, had a tough first year. An ageing team finished just one place off the bottom and had to take part in the Victorian version of Play-Offs, or 'Test Matches', as they were known. Together with bottom of the table Burnley, they took part in home and away fixtures with Notts County and Newton Heath (later Man Utd), who had finished as the top two in the Second Division.

An opening defeat against Notts County was followed by draws with both of the Second

Division hopefuls, which meant that nothing but victory in the final game with Newton Heath would suffice. In what can be considered a farewell performance, 'The Team' showed their talent one last time to win 2-0 and preserve the top-flight status the club would jealously guard until 1958, when the proud boast of being the only club never to play anything but top flight football was ended.

As the era of the club's most successful team drew to a close, new impetus for the club was being created with the building of Roker Park, barely a quarter of a mile away from the Newcastle Road ground that had been captured forever in Thomas M. Hemy's painting of a match with Aston Villa. Believed to be the world's oldest oil painting of an association football match, the huge canvas now takes pride of place in the entrance to the Stadium of Light.

The last of a dozen seasons at Newcastle Road saw the team undergo a transformation in personnel, although Doig and Wilson survived from the treble title winning side. They were instrumental in helping achieve the best defensive record in the division and largely because of it, the runners-up spot behind Sheffield United's only Championship team.

Newcastle Road hosted its last match on St. George's Day 1897, when former Bolton Wanderer, Jimmy Leslie, claimed the ground's final goal in a 4-0 farewell. Sunderland had been in existence for less than two decades, had won the title three times, tasted FA Cup semi-final disappointment as often, had established a hatful of records and including the brief flirtation with a pitch at The Cedars, had had seven homes. Most importantly of all, 'The Team of All The Talents' had provided Sunderland with a team whose achievements could forever stand comparison with the legendary teams that would dominate football in the twentieth century.

DOUBLE TROUBLE 1898 - World War One (1898-1918)

Having scored the final goal at the Newcastle Road ground, Jimmy Leslie imprinted his name indelibly on the club's history by also registering the first ever goal at Roker Park, six minutes before the end of the opening game, to give a 1-0 win over Liverpool. The opening game was played on September 10th 1898 but originally the ground had been due to open on August 12th. The delay was due to the unavailability of the Marquis of Londonderry, who was to open the ground. Nonetheless, a crowd of around 14,000 turned up on the original opening date for an 'Olympic Games' event. The modern Olympics had been revived in 1896 and this was the second 'Olympic' event staged by the club. However, unlike the real Olympics, Sunderland offered prize money, with £250 in all to be won and a top prize of £20 for the 110 yards. There was also £5 on offer in a dribbling contest – perhaps an indication of the future value of athleticism over artistry.

The club's first chairman J. P. Henderson was the leading figure in ensuring the move to Roker Park. The land that was to become the most important part of Sunderland for a century was farmland belonging to a Mr Tennant. Initially, the ground was leased, with the deal dependent on J.P. Henderson agreeing to supply a building layout for plans to construct houses in the area surrounding the new ground.

The stadium took less than a year to build, with the wooden stands taking three months to erect. Capacity was said to be 34,000 with the Grandstand claimed to have 3,000 seats, although the more reliable 1914 figure of 2,450 is more likely to be accurate. The ends were both uncovered and were known as the North and South Ends, with the North (later Fulwell) also known as the Top End. A century later, the Stadium of Light would also begin life with Ends initially named North and South. Roker Park would always be renowned for the quality of its playing surface, which began with the import of finest quality Irish turf that was so good, it was thirty years until it was relayed.

When the serious business of football began at the new ground, the town's enthusiasm for the sport was much in evidence. J.P. Henderson was the son of the originator of the Corporation Steam Ferry and on Roker Park's opening, a pair of steamboats paraded up river, while a pipe band marched from the town to the ground. Flags flew over a huge crowd of 30,000, which beat Newcastle Road's record of 23,000, which itself was 5,000 over the former home's supposed capacity.

The Marquis of Londonderry opened the ground with a golden key that unlocked a gate leading to the dressing rooms. In charge of Liverpool was none other than Tom Watson, the former secretary/manager of 'The Team of All the Talents.'

Sunderland wore white shirts for the opening game at Roker Park. The team was: Doig, Bach, McNeil, Ferguson, McAllister, Wilson, Crawford, Leslie, Morgan, Chalmers and Saxton. Liverpool lined up: Storer, A. Goldie, Dunlop, Howell, Raisbeck, W. Goldie, Cox, Walker, Allan, Morgan and Robertson.

Sunderland finished seventh in their first year at Roker Park, where they won six and drew one of their first seven games. Everton's Laurie Bell became the first visiting player to score (in the sixth match), while Burnley completed a notable double by being the first visiting side to leave Roker with maximum points, eight years after winning on Wearside in Sunderland's first ever league game.

Christmas Eve 1898 saw Newcastle's first visit to Roker Park, when a crowd of 25,000 found that admission prices had been raised, which wasn't the best of Christmas presents to supporters who were further dismayed when the 'Magpies' won 3-2. That man Leslie scored twice but goals from Wardrope and Peddie, who got two, put United in command. The club justified the inflated prices by stating that the increase in revenue was so that a roof could be put on the Press Box. Presumably this was one way of deflecting press criticism! Not surprisingly, Leslie finished Roker's first season as top scorer, with ten goals, average attendance for the first season being 13,863.

The club was soon awarded a full international fixture and on February 18th 1899 England rattled up what remains their record home victory, when Northern Ireland were trounced 13-2.

In England's record home win at Roker, G. O. Smith of Corinthians scored four times. Man Utd's Gary and Phil Neville played together for England against China in 1996 and in so doing became only the second brothers from the same league club to play alongside each other for England. Nottingham Forest's Fred and Frank Forman not only played together at Roker against Ireland but they both scored!

The game marked the only international appearance of Sunderland's Phil Bach but his cap cost him his Sunderland place, as, while 13,000 watched England at Roker, Sunderland beat Sheffield Wednesday at Hillsborough, where newly-signed Andrew McCombie did so well, Bach couldn't regain his place in the side. Bach was Sunderland's second England cap (Tom Porteous v Wales in 1891 being the first) and he later became chairman of his first club, Middlesbrough and an international selector.

Manager, Robert Campbell, left at the end of the first season at Roker and has the unenviable record of being Sunderland's only pre-Second World War manager not to win the Championship, although one runners-up position in a three-year transitional spell both on and off the pitch was, perhaps, not a bad record.

Alex Mackie was his successor. Only 29 when appointed, Mackie had never played professionally but had been with several Scottish clubs. He was in charge for six seasons, during which the club never finished outside the top six and took the title again in 1902. Mackie based his game on defence. Only 35 goals were conceded in the 34-game Championship season, yet this was nine more than a year earlier when 'The Lads' were runners-up. Centre half, Sandy McAllister, had been the only ever-present in the opening year at Roker Park and also became the Championship side's only ever-present. A popular player with the supporters, they promised to buy him a piano if he scored and when he eventually did, they not only provided his piano but gave him a gold watch, too!

A single point stopped Sunderland retaining the title a year later, when a calamitous home defeat by eventual champions, Sheffield Wednesday, cost more than lost points. Roker Park was closed following an attack on the Wednesday bus afterwards, which meant that Sunderland's first ever home league derby with Middlesbrough was played at St James Park. Although that match was won, 'The Lads' lost on the same ground to Newcastle a week later when, Bob McColl (who later founded the McColl's newsagent chain) scored the winner to end Sunderland's 100% league record on Tyneside.

Missing from that game through injury were McCallister and defender, Andy McCombie, who had followed Doig and Wilson in becoming the third Sunderland player to be capped by Scotland. McCombie later became embroiled in a dispute with the club over a matter of £100 that he was unhappy to discover had been a loan rather than a gift. The case ended up in court, where it was ruled to be a loan but an FA enquiry into the club's affairs followed in October and Sunderland duly became one of seven clubs to be punished for financial irregularities during the decade. Found guilty of paying bonuses, Sunderland were fined £250 and had six directors suspended for two and a half years.

Manager Mackie was suspended for three months. After resuming his duties he sold Alf Common to Middlesbrough in the game's first ever £1,000 transfer and four months later moved to 'Boro himself. Mackie had previously sold Common to Sheffield United and had re-signed him. At Ayresome, Alex Mackie was again found guilty of financial irregularites and suspended, after which he left the game to become a publican. McCombie, meanwhile, had moved on for £700 to Newcastle, against whom he scored an own goal on his return to Roker.

Mackie's successor at Roker Park was Robert H. Kyle, who was in control as secretary/manager from 1905 until 1928, making him Sunderland's longest-serving manager. He came close to winning the double in 1913 but then saw the First World War deny his side the opportunity of further success. Throughout Bob Kyle's, era he had Billy Williams as trainer. Williams provided a link with the old Newcastle Road days, having served the club since 1897.

Kyle's reign began with a 3-2 home win over Newcastle but his first three years proved difficult, with the club finishing 14th, 10th and 16th, whereas only once previously had they finished lower than seventh and in over half of the seasons since joining the league, Sunderland had been in the top three. However, a Championship team was being assembled, while off the pitch, Roker Park was purchased for £10,000 by the club, which became a limited company in 1906.

Legendary goalkeeper, L.R. Roose and stalwart centre half, Charlie Thompson, arrived in 1908 · a year that for Sunderland supporters will forever be synonymous with a 9-1 away win over Newcastle, still the joint record top-flight away victory. At the end of that season the club undertook its inaugural overseas tour to Hungary, Austria, Germany and Czechoslovakia, losing just once and winning seven times.

From 1910 to 1912, Sunderland finished 8th, 3rd and 8th, with the immortal Charlie Buchan, who went on to score more league goals (209) for the club than any other player, signing from Leyton in 1911. Since the Championship year of 1902, Sunderland hadn't won a major honour for a decade but all that was soon to change.

Seven games into the 1912-13 campaign, Sunderland were bottom of the table and without a win; but after signing goalkeeper, Joe Butler and right back, Charlie Gladwin, from Second Division Glossop and Blackpool, fortunes began to turn. The title was taken, with the 54-point total representing the best of any club before the introduction of the 42 game season. Charlie Buchan became the first of three players to score five times in a league game for Sunderland (also Gurney 1935 & Sharkey 1963) when Liverpool went down 7-0 at Roker. 'The Lads' also reached their first FA Cup Final, only to go down 1-0 to Aston Villa.

Villa and Sunderland denied each other the double. Four days after the cup final, Sunderland beat runners-up Villa 1-0 at Villa Park, where Walter Tinsley got the winner and Sunderland hit the woodwork three times. Tinsley should have played in the cup final but was too nervous to appear at Crystal Palace in front of the record 120,081 crowd, which has only ever been surpassed in England by the first Wembley Final a decade later. Only three men have scored more goals for Sunderland than George Holley who had scored the winner in the semi final replay with Burnley but the injured Holley became a virtual passenger when forced to turn out in the Final after Tinsley's withdrawal. Geordie Clem Stephenson, of Villa, had dreamt that Villa would win 1-0 with a goal from Tommy Barber and this proved to be the case, with Villa's Sunderland born Charlie Wallace missing a penalty.

The cup run had taken in a controversial abandoned match at Manchester City, twenty fans being injured when falling from the roof of the Roker Coal Depot as they tried to see the replay and a three match quarter final with Newcastle, who were eventually overcome when Sunderland inflicted only their second home cup defeat in seventeen years.

In 1914, the cup quarter final was reached only for eventual winners, Burnley, to triumph in a replay, while in the league a moderate 7th place was achieved. Despite the outbreak of World War One, the 1914-15 season was not only started but completed, with Sunderland finishing 8th. The final league game before the league was suspended saw Spurs defeated 5-0 at Roker, with the obligatory Buchan hat trick.

The suspension of league football marked the end of what was a hugely successful era for the red and whites. In twenty-five seasons since their election to the league, the club had taken the title five times and finished outside the top ten on only three occasions.

CUP WINNERS AT LAST - INTER WAR YEARS (1918-1939)

Compared to the trophy-laden pre-WW1 era, the inter-war years were mainly barren until shortly before war broke out again. Prior to the Football League resuming in 1919-20, Sunderland participated in what was dubbed the 'Victory League' between January and April 1919. The competition was between eight north east clubs and began for Sunderland with a 1-0 defeat at Durham City.

Charlie Buchan was quick off the mark when the Football League recommenced. He scored in the opening 2-1 win over Aston Villa and majestically resumed his role as scorer supreme. Between 1913 and 1924, Buchan was top scorer in every season played and in 1923 was the First Division's leading marksman. Goodness knows by how much he would have extended his club record goals haul if the war hadn't intervened.

Inevitably clubs had to build new sides and in the summer of 1920, Jackie Mordue's move to Middlesbrough broke up Sunderland's renowned right-wing combination of Buchan, Mordue and Cuggy, which was as famous as the 1990's Arsenal defence that began to be dismantled with Steve Bould's move to Sunderland.

Fifth place was achieved in the first post-war season but both 1921 and 1922 saw 'The Lads' finish in a disappointing 12th position. Bob Kyle spent around £25,000 in March 1922 bringing in four players to boost the side. Of these, the most influential proved to be full back, Warney Cresswell, whose brother Frank later played briefly alongside him. Buchan eventually moved on to Arsenal in 1925 for an initial fee of £2,000, which was more than doubled after he scored 21 goals in his first season, with 'The Gunners' having promised Sunderland a further £100 for every goal scored in his first year at Highbury. Buchan's name remained prominent for decades after his retirement, partly through his long running magazine, 'Charles Buchan's Football Monthly.'

Although trophies eluded the club throughout the twenties, a five-year spell between 1923 and 1927 saw 'The Lads' rated as one of the country's leading sides as three third-place finishes and a runners-up spot were achieved, with a placing of seventh in the middle of that spell. The FA Cup continued to be a source of frustration, though, with the club never roaring beyond the fifth round during the twenties.

W. Cresswell

Sunderland had England's Charlie Buchan and Scotland's Billy Clunas facing each other in Wembley's first international in 1924, four years after Roker Park had again been used to host an England v Ireland full international. The developing Roker Park was again chosen for a major fixture in 1926, when Northern Nomads beat Stockton 7-1 in the FA Amateur Cup Final. The Amateur Cup Final returned to Roker thirteen years later, when Hetton-born Bob Paisley, who later led Liverpool to European Cup glory, was in the Bishop Auckland side that beat Willington 3-0.

While the mid-twenties team never scaled the heights of several previous Sunderland sides, they did achieve a fair standard of consistency in the higher echelon of the league table. Rather like the 'Team of All the Talents' from three decades earlier, though, they aged as a side, only to produce one last great effort to prevent the club slipping out of the top flight. Although 15th place was fairly respectable on paper, only one point separated Sunderland from relegated Spurs in 21st spot.

Bottom of the table 'Boro could have saved themselves if they'd drawn with Sunderland at Ayresome Park on the last day of the season, while, because of an inferior goal average, the Wearsiders needed to win. The showdown took place forty five years to the day before Sunderland's epic 1973 FA Cup triumph over Leeds United at Wembley. That day is remembered by many for Jimmy Montgomery's classic double save and it was another Sunderland goalkeeping great who produced his own heroics, including a never-to-be-forgotten double stop from 'Boro's Carr and Bruce. Albert McInroy had arrived at Sunderland five years earlier, after Bob Kyle signed him in a Manchester toilet at midnight, a minute after his contract with Leyland Motors expired. It was one of Kyle's best acquisitions · McInroy remains the only Sunderland goalkeeper to win a full cap for England and he played the proverbial 'blinder' to keep Sunderland up in the do-or-die meeting with Middlesbrough. Appropriately, perhaps, Billy Death, in his last game for the club, became one of the scorers, as Sunderland went on to win 3-0 after 'Albert the Great,' as McInroy was known, had blunted 'Boro.

Also on the mark that day was David Halliday. He had arrived from Dundee in the summer of 1925 and took over from Buchan, whom he would ultimately follow to Highbury. Halliday was a phenomenal goalscorer, playing in an age when defences were having to adjust to a new offside rule. Halliday stayed only four seasons but only Buchan and Bobby Gurney, who succeeded Halliday, have scored more goals for Sunderland.

Dave Halliday scored more goals in his poorest full season than any other Sunderland player has ever scored in their best season (excluding wartime records)! The Scot hit 42 league and cup goals in 1925-26, 36 a year later, 39 in 1927-28, a record 43 1928-29 and 4 in 11 games before his £6,000 move to Arsenal in November 1929. Altogether, his 164 goals came in 175 games. Halliday's career total of league goals was a phenomenal 334 in 447 matches. In 1958, as manager of Leicester, he would see his side's end-of-season win over Birmingham effectively finally relegate Sunderland for the first time.

Halliday's record season of 1928-29 was manager, Johnny Cochrane's, first. Helped by Halliday's haul, Sunderland finished fourth. Roker Park's famous Archibald Leitch–designed Main Stand, with the distinctive crisscross latticework, also seen at Ibrox, Goodison and Fratton Park, was opened in September 1929 and seven years later, Leitch's Clock Stand was opened, giving Roker Park the essential shape it took for the rest of its time, with only the roofing of the Fulwell End for the 1966 World Cup significantly changing its shape as the ground grew old with the century.

The thirties were to end Sunderland's wait for a sixth Championship and at last bring the FA Cup to Wearside. The cup semi final was reached in 1931 and two years later, cup fever brought a record 75,118 into Roker for a quarter-final replay with Derby County. Cochrane gradually assembled his side, which finished the first four years of the thirties stuck in mid table.

Players such as Raich Carter, Bobby Gurney, Patsy Gallacher, Jimmy Connor and Charlie Thomson were gelling together as a great side and Arsenal's dominance was threatened as Sunderland climbed the table, finishing 6th in 1934, runners-up in 1935 and finally, champions again in 1936. Many consider the December 1935, 5-4 win over Arsenal, the greatest game ever seen at Roker. Carter scored twice in the match, although Gurney surprisingly didn't get on the scoresheet. The pair finished as joint top scorers, with 31 each, Gurney hitting four in a 7-2 away win over Birmingham City that clinched the title with three games to spare.

Full back Harold Shaw - the only ever-present in 1931-32.

As the 1936 Championship was secured, Aston Villa and Blackburn Rovers quietly slipped out of the First Division. Their relegation meant that champions, Sunderland, were now the only club who had never played outside of the top flight. It would be more than two decades before that claim was put to rest.

Raich Carter may well have been the finest footballer ever to pull on the red and white shirt. A brilliant inside forward who also excelled at international level, Carter's collection of medals and shirts were bought by Sunderland Council in the 1990s for display in The Raich Carter Centre built in his native Hendon. Gurney was also Sunderland-born, hailing from Silksworth. He was a player who fought for every ball and his 228 league and cup goals make him the highest ever scorer in the club's history (Buchan is the highest league scorer). Gurney once scored nine times in a reserve match and he became only the second player to score five in a league game for Sunderland. His only full England cap came in 1935 - a year after he scored twice at Roker against England for 'The Rest' in a trial match, when Carter hit four as England were beaten 7-1!

The Championship success was tinged with sadness, though, as diabetic goalkeeper, Jimmy Thorpe, died in hospital after being injured in a fiercely contested late-season match with Chelsea at Roker. Teenager, Johnny Mapson, was signed from Reading to replace him and a year later, he became the youngest FA Cup Final goalkeeper (a record beaten by Peter Shilton in 1969) when he played on the day before his twentieth birthday. Mapson reported an attempt by Wolves to bribe him in a quarter final that went to three games before Third Division Millwall were disposed of in the semi final at Huddersfield, where Gurney and Gallacher goals overturned a deficit caused by Millwall's Dave Mangnall.

Sunderland also had to come from behind to beat Preston North End at Wembley. Gurney and Carter overturned Preston's lead, given to them on the stroke of half time by Frank O'Donnell and three minutes from time, left winger, Eddie Burbanks, made it 3-1 to at last fulfil all Wearside's desire to be cup holders.

Success in the cup was more than adequate compensation for finishing only eighth just a year after being champions. The following year, the same position and even the number of points were repeated but hopes that the cup win would be emulated, too, were dashed at the semi-final stage. In the final season before the war, a miserable 16th place equalled the club's lowest ever position (1908) and Johnny Cochrane stepped down as manager, to be replaced by Bill Murray. Murray had played over 300 games for Sunderland, including half of the 1936 Championship campaign and also the famous last-day win to avoid relegation at Middlesbrough in 1928. The 1939-40 season began but war broke out the day after the third game of the season, when Ted Drake scored four against Sunderland for Arsenal in a 5-1 Highbury defeat.

At the outbreak of war, Sunderland were a giant of the game but in the years afterwards, despite splashing out what was, for the time, giant wads of cash, the giant that was Sunderland gradually fell into a deep sleep.

FINAL TIE

OF THE
FOOTBALL
ASSOCIATION
CHALLENGE CUP
COMPETITION

AT THE

EMPIRE STADIUM
WEMBLEY

SATURDAY, MAY 1, 1937

CORONATION YEAR OF THEIR MAJESTIES
KING GEORGE VI AND QUEEN ELIZABETH

PRESTON NORTH END
v.
SUNDERLAND
Kick-off 3 p.m.

OFFICIAL PROGRAMME SIXPENCE

The cover of the 1937 Cup Final programme.

DECLINE OF THE BANK OF ENGLAND CLUB
(1939 - 1958).

Football struggled on during the war years, with Roker Park suffering bomb damage in 1943. In 1941, a North League was set up, Sunderland kicking off with a Raich Carter hat-trick in a 7-1 win over Sheffield United. In all, thirty games were played that season, with Carter hitting two more hat-tricks, while Cliff Whitelum twice got four. Whitelum surpassed this a year later, when he scored all six at Roker Park in the first leg of the West Riding FA Cup Final, when Huddersfield were thrashed 6-2. Sunderland took the trophy 7-6 on aggregate. Whitelum's wartime total for 'The Lads' was 133 goals in 165 games, including a phenomenal 41 goals in 36 games in 1944-45. Having played twice before the war as a youngster, Whitelum played briefly afterwards, averaging a goal every two games in 1946-47.

Wartime teams included many 'guest' players and even Newcastle legend, Albert Stubbins, turned out for Sunderland, scoring for the Wearsiders (with Carter) in the 1942 War Cup Final first leg with Wolves at Roker, which was drawn 2-2, before 'The Lads' went down 4-1 at Molineux.

The FA Cup began before the Football League resumed after the war. Beginning in January 1946, cup ties were played over two legs, Sunderland beginning the post-war era with a 3-1 win at Grimsby. Raich Carter played in Roker's opening post-war league game the following August but sadly, he was by then with Derby County. Sunderland benefited from the continuing service of pre-war players like Mapson, Burbanks, Arthur Wright and Len Duns but manager Bill Murray, who had taken over just before the war, faced the task of rebuilding the side.

The first big signing was Willie Watson, who represented England at cricket as well as football. Centre half, Fred Hall, arrived from Blackburn and became a great Sunderland captain. A reasonable placing of 9th was managed on the resumption of league football but in 1948, Sunderland skirted dangerously close to relegation, as they had in 1897 and 1928.

Four successive home wins at the end of the season kept the club up after the 'Clown Prince of Soccer', Len Shackleton, had been signed from Newcastle in February. The scorer of six goals on his debut for the Magpies, 'Shack' had a less auspicious start to life with Sunderland in a 5-1 defeat at Derby but after scoring on his home debut, he went on to become a Roker immortal. Only Gary Rowell has since matched Shack's post- war century of goals for Sunderland and up to the start of the 1999-2000 season, Shack remains the last Sunderland player to score for England. However, facts and statistics don't show Shack's greatness, they merely illustrate that, behind the legendary tales of his showmanship, he evidently produced the goods more often than not. Later to open the club's Visitor Centre when the Stadium of Light started to be built, Shack remains ever popular on Wearside, not least for his oft-stated opinion that he has no prejudice where Newcastle are concerned - he says he's not bothered who beats them!

Although things started to improve in the late forties, with a top-half finish in 1949, that season is inevitably linked with the club's greatest ever cup disaster. If Sunderland were approaching the time when they would become known as a Sleeping Giant, it's arguable that non-league Yeovil administered the sleeping pill, when knocking Sunderland out of the FA Cup in a first game that went straight into extra time.

Within 48 hours, Sunderland responded by signing Ivor Broadis in a peculiar transfer where the Carlisle player/manager (who would go on to play for England) transferred himself! Winger, Tommy Wright, soon followed, as Sunderland continued to spend in the search for success.

Massive crowds gave an aggregate for the season of over a million spectators, with an average gate of 47,785 when a title challenge was based on strong home form. One slip in that home record cost the Championship, though, when relegation-doomed Manchester City inflicted a late-season defeat, leaving Sunderland ultimately third, a point behind champions, Portsmouth.

Disappointed, Sunderland became known as 'The Bank of England Club' as the cheque book was brandished. Welsh international, Trevor Ford, arrived for a record £29,500 despite the fact that existing centre forward, Dickie Davis, had just finished as the First Division's leading scorer. In the same month that Ford arrived, a further £9,000 was spent on winger, Billy Bingham, who in 1958 became the only player to play in the World Cup Finals while on Sunderland's books and in 1982 managed Northern Ireland's celebrated World Cup team in Spain.

Trevor Ford scored a hat-trick and even managed to dislodge a goalpost on his home debut. A month later, he scored twice for Wales in a 4-2 defeat by England, who included Willie Watson in England's last full international at Roker Park. Ford scored 70 goals in 117 games in three years, before Sunderland got their money back on him with a transfer to Cardiff. Ford and Shackleton were two of Sunderland's greatest ever forwards but they famously failed to hit it off together, either on or off the pitch.

Following consecutive 12th place finishes, Bill Murray's team challenged for the title in 1953, topping the table in December, a month when floodlit football came to Roker, Dundee being the first nightime opponents, closely followed by glamorous Racing Club Paris. Whereas a good finish had fended off relegation five years earlier, here a terrible second half of the season saw 'The Lads' plummet to 9th.

This wasn't good enough for either the board or the supporters and so at the end of this spell, a spending spree of £70,000 on three players inside a month resulted in the 'Bank of England Club' label and provided national debate of the sort that bankrolled Blackburn endured in the mid-1990s. The trio of big signings were goalkeeper, Jimmy Cowan, centre half, Ray Daniel and hard man, Billy Elliott, who played in all the left-flank positions for Sunderland. One home-grown player who made his debut during the season was Stan Anderson, who became the first outfield player to top 400 appearances for the club.

In 1972, Billy Elliott had a spell as caretaker manager, converting Dave Watson to a centre half and later that season, Elliott was trainer under Bob Stokoe when the cup was won. Six years later, Elliott's lengthy spell as caretaker boss saw the club just miss out on promotion. Elliott was still watching Sunderland in 1999, having recovered from a suspected heart attack while at the ground in the record-breaking promotion season.

Ray Daniels

Hopes that the newcomers would improve things were dashed as the team struggled badly. Top twelve months earlier, 'The Lads' propped up the table, with a clean sheet still to be achieved and several heavy defeats already suffered, when Santa arrived in 1953. A set of individuals rather than a team, they occasionally clicked spectacularly, such as when inflicting Arsenal's record post-war defeat, Ford nabbing a hat-trick, with all but Bingham of the all-international front five scoring as the Gunners were walloped 7-1.

Ford departed soon afterwards but Murray continued to make more signings than an early-eighties dole office, with Ken Chisholm, Ted Purdon, Joe McDonald and goalkeeper, Willie Fraser, coming in as the team climbed away from the dreaded drop.

There was an overdue upturn in 1954-55, when a top-four place was achieved for only the second (and to date, last) time since the 1936 Championship season. The semi final of the FA Cup was also reached for the first time since the war, with Chisholm and Purdon leading the way in the cup goalscoring stakes, while Shack, Elliott and new boy, Charlie 'Cannonball' Fleming, also made their mark. Five years earlier, Manchester City had cost Sunderland the league title by winning at Roker and on a very heavy pitch at Villa Park, they ended Wearside cup hopes.

Those hopes were particularly special, because a win would have set up a Cup Final meeting with Newcastle, who progressed to Wembley after winning in Roker Park's only FA Cup semi final, in which they defeated York City in a replay.

The Magpies won the cup and the following year did the 'double' over Sunderland, including a record Newcastle win on Wearside, with a 6-1 Boxing Day scoreline. Sunderland slipped to 9th in the league but reached the cup semi again, gaining revenge on Newcastle by knocking the holders out on their own patch in the quarter final. Sunderland, though, were comprehensively beaten 3-0 by Birmingham City at Hillsborough and wouldn't progress so far again until winning on the same ground in 1973. Throughout the mid-fifties, the club cheque book was never allowed to gather dust, with Bill Holden who scored twice in the cup win at Newcastle, Don Revie and Colin Grainger among those coming in.

The club's long-cherished record of being the only club never to play outside the top division was again put under severe strain in 1956-57, when only good late season form avoided the drop but off the pitch there were even greater problems.

The Football League were tipped off by someone who never came forward but signed himself "Smith", that Sunderland had been making illegal payments. This was still the age of the maximum wage and Sunderland certainly weren't the only club making illegal payments, as several players made clear; but the club were severely punished in a case reminiscent of the 1904 scandal involving manager, Alex Mackie and the board.

Found guilty of making illegal payments, half a dozen players were banned for not co-operating with the FA Commission, although the punishment was lifted a month later, when the players accepted that illegal payments had been made but disagreed about the amounts. Of the players involved, Ford and Chisholm had left Sunderland but Elliott, Daniel, Fraser and Johnny Hannigan were still at the club.

Sunderland chairman, Ted Ditchburn and director, Martin were permanently suspended. Vice-chairman, Ritson and fellow-director, Martin, received sine-die suspensions, while the rest of the board were warned. Five years later, the High Court overruled the decision on Ditchburn. There was also a £5,000 fine and expenses for the club to contend with.

Later, ten more players were implicated in the scandal and were financially punished by the Commission. Manager, Bill Murray, was fined only £200 when it was taken into account that he was a pawn in the game but having been manager since before the war and having first played for the club in 1927, it was a sad ending and he resigned soon after.

Having broken the bank at 'The Bank of England Club', there was a shift of policy following the punishment for financial irregularities. Considering that, in years to come, Sunderland were to be promoted ahead of Swindon Town as the Wiltshire club's punishment for financial irregularities, it could be argued that Sunderland got off lightly. In fact, though, Sunderland finally went down the following season, ending a record unbroken 68 years and 57-season-long residency at the peak of English football.

Following the appointment of Alan Brown as manager, the club changed from trying to buy ready-made talent, to trying to produce more of it's own, although Brown still was given substantial funds and made several forays into the transfer market as the team went through a period of rapid transition.

An opening-day defeat at home to Arsenal marked Shack's retirement and things went from bad to worse, as between four and seven goals were conceded on no fewer than eight occasions. Two huge seven and six nil hammerings marked the beginning of the career of the player supporters would later vote as their Player of the Century. Cork-born but London-raised Charlie Hurley was bought from Millwall. Brown had been an imposing centre half himself and knew what he was looking for. 'Bomber' Brown was prepared to build a team in his image but couldn't stop them sliding into the Second Division.

Sunderland needed to win on the final day of the season at Portsmouth and hope that Leicester would lose in order for the Wearsiders to stay up. Two goals from South African, Don Kichenbrand, gave Sunderland a win but they still went down on goal average as Leicester, managed by Sunderland scoring legend, Dave Halliday, also won, to condemn Wearsiders to Second Division football they would see far too much of in the years to come.

BROWNED OFF
(1958-1972)

Being in the Second Division took some getting used to, both for the supporters and the team. Hannigan, Fleming, Bingham and Scottish international fullback Joe McDonald, moved on, while Revie also sought a transfer and was duly left out of the side before he eventually moved on to Leeds. His path and Sunderland's would, of course, cross again. Humbled 3-1 at Lincoln City in the opening game, Sunderland found it difficult to adjust and by the end of September they were bottom of the table, having conceded six (twice) and five in three successive away games. Brown's clearout continued, with Fraser and fellow Scottish international, George Aitken, who had been a stalwart of the side throughout the fifties, joining the exodus of big-name stars. Goalkeeper, Peter Wakeham, arrived and an increasing amount of faith in young players brought in the likes of Len Ashurst, Jimmy McNab and sixteen-year-old Cec Irwin, who would all go on to give sterling service.

Throughout this time, the hub of the side was Horden-born Stan Anderson who, missed only five games in the first four years out of the top flight, as he fought to inspire 'The Lads' to former glories. Such glories seemed a long way off as Sunderland scraped miserable 15th and 16th places in their first two Second Division sojourns. Hope started to build, though, in the 1960-1961 season. Sixth place at least offered a glimpse of promotion and in the cups, Sunderland started to show the big boys that they could still be a force to be reckoned with, despite a 4-3 defeat at the hands of Brentford in the club's first ever League Cup tie.

Any cup fever found in Sunderland required the symptom of it being the FA Cup and when Arsenal arrived at Roker in the 3rd round, a crowd of 58,575 saw wing half Anderson score twice as the Gunners were beaten. Just over a year later, Anderson would earn two England caps but had he been in the First Division, or at a southern club, he would surely have earned more. The cup run continued with away wins at Liverpool and Norwich, before the quarter-final draw brought Tottenham to Roker.

Spurs were en route to becoming the first club this century to do the 'double' (If only Sunderland could have won the 1913 Cup Final!) and the famed Roker Roar was in full voice as 'The Lads' ripped into the Londoners. Over sixty thousand made so much noise that Spurs' esteemed Danny Blanchflower was convinced the noise was amplified through loudspeakers. It wasn't of course - it was inspired, as it always has been, by passion and pride and that pride was being re-kindled and was felt more deeply after the terrible years the club and supporters had been through.

By now, Charlie Hurley was playing as a Player of the Century should. "Charlie, Charlie", became the crowd's mantra whenever a corner was given. 'The King', as Hurley was known, had scored the fifth round winner at Norwich to set up the Spurs tie. Spurs' push-and-run style took them into an early lead but no longer the pushovers they'd been in recent years, Sunderland stormed back to equalise. Willie McPheat levelled after four corners in quick succession had put the country's best side under pressure. The Official History of Tottenham Hotspur describes the goal as, "Perhaps the single most worrying moment during the 'Double' season." Although Spurs' class told in the replay, when they hit five without reply, it didn't alter the fact that Sunderland were evidently improving.

The summer signing of Brian Clough meant that the improvement gathered pace. Outrage was caused, though, by the decision to change the colour of the team's shorts to white. In a season when Jimmy Montgomery started to break through into the first team, Sunderland started to look as if they could get back into the First Division. Seven successive wins meant that, come the final game of the season at Swansea, a win could take them up. Both Clough and Ambrose Fogarty had hit hat tricks in the reverse fixture, which had been won 7-2 but the match was only drawn and Sunderland had to settle for third place in the days when only the top two went up.

Going for it, Sunderland brought in Northern Ireland forward, Johnny Crossan and Scotland winger, George Mulhall and there were plenty of other newcomers as well on the terraces, where the average crowd topped 40,000, having been barely half that four years earlier.

The 1962-63 season turned on two players called Harker and Harmer. The former was the Bury goalkeeper involved in a Boxing Day collision that wrecked Cloughie's career, while Chelsea's Tommy Harmer certainly harmed Sunderland in the final game of the season, when he scored the only goal at Roker on a day when a point would have guaranteed promotion.

Best known now as a manager, Brian Clough had a phenomenal goalscoring record at both Sunderland and his home town, Middlesbrough, from whom Sunderland bought him for £42,000. 204 goals in 222 games on Teesside had brought him two England caps and his 63 goals in 74 Sunderland games included 28 goals in as many games in the half-season up to his injury. Over a year later, he tried to make a comeback and scored once in his only three First Division games. In 1966, over 30,000 turned up for his testimonial at Roker Park. He coached the Sunderland youth team before moving into management with Hartlepool. Despite stating that he would walk to Sunderland if appointed manager and the desire among the fans for him to do for Sunderland what he did for Derby and Forest - at one point it seemed as if every car on Wearside carried a 'Get Clough for Roker' sticker - he never got the chance.

Nick Sharkey did as well as anyone could be expected to in filling Clough's boots. He averaged better than a goal every two games in well over a hundred appearances by the time he left in 1966. In his fifth league game after replacing Clough, he became the third (and to date, last) Sunderland player to score five times in a match. He also netted Sunderland's goal in a 3-1 aggregate defeat by Aston Villa in the club's first ever League Cup semi final, while in the FA Cup that year, he was one of the scorers against Gravesend & Northfleet on the last occasion Sunderland met non-league cup opposition.

With the club *on* the up, it was inevitable that they would *go* up and so it proved in 1964, when, as runners-up to Leeds, Sunderland got back to the division they thought of as their rightful home. A settled side included four ever-presents and another five players who missed no more than five games. Former goalkeeper, Peter Wakeham, played a 'blinder' for opponents, Charlton, at Roker on the day promotion was sealed, with Crossan converting Mulhall's last-minute cross for a winner that sparked scenes of unheralded joy and the most emotional lap of honour as 'The King' was carried before his subjects.

Ironically, given the obsession people had with promotion, the highlight of the season came in the cup. The gates were forced as crowds believed to number more than Roker's official record of 75,118 piled in to see a quarter-final replay with Manchester United, three years to the day since Spurs had faced the Roker Roar. Jimmy Montgomery was in the process of proving he was, 'The Mighty Jim' and was in the

Souvenir cover of the promotion year brochure for 1964.

middle of a run in which he was beaten only once in nine league games. In the first tie at Old Trafford, he had been beaten twice in the last four minutes, with Charlton and Best pulling United back for a 3-3 draw after Monty had been injured. A third replay was needed after Bobby Charlton saved United again two minutes from the end of extra time. As with the Spurs tie, Sunderland finally came a cropper but not before showing they were ready to take on the best.

Four years later, Man Utd beat Benfica to win the European Cup. Like United, Benfica also played at Roker in 1963-64, Sunderland putting five past the team who play at the original Stadium of Light. A week earlier, Stan Anderson had moved on to Newcastle as Martin Harvey established himself at Sunderland.

As with the 1999 promotion, the fans were on the crest of a wave, only to come off their surfboard when the club threatened to run aground in the close season. Whereas in 1999 it was the transfer listing of three talented players that dampened spirits, in 1964 it was the sudden departure of manager, Alan Brown, that caused problems which were exacerbated when Montgomery was injured, leaving fifteen-year-old goalkeeper, Derek Forster, to play in the first match back in the top flight.

Imagine putting a fifteen-year-old in goal these days to face the likes of Zola or Beckham – but Forster was no mug. He'd played in front of 99,000 at Wembley for England schoolboys and had been chosen ahead of reserve 'keeper, Derek Kirby, by trainers Arthur Wright and Jack Jones, who were in temporary charge of the team. Nonetheless, a glance at the opposition goalkeeper, Leicester and England's Gordon Banks, illustrated the challenge facing Sunderland on their First Division return. Honours ended even in a 3-3 draw and although only one of the opening fifteen games was won, fifteenth place was managed by the end of the campaign. In November, former England international, George Hardwick, was appointed manager after a spell coaching Middlesbrough but perhaps harshly, his services were dispensed with at the end of the season.

His replacement was former Scotland manager, Ian McColl. He spent £340,000 on nine new players, including Jim Baxter from Rangers. Like Baxter, McColl had been a wing half at Ibrox and indeed had played over 400 games for Rangers. Baxter was a world-class star, as he proved on his home debut against Sheffield United. 'Slim' Jim equalised the Blades' early opener, before putting Sunderland ahead with a magnificent goal, for which he ran from his own half, traded passes and finished from the edge of the box. He really turned it on in a 4-1 win but such performances were to be the exception rather than the rule, as he often didn't live up to his star billing.

Alan Gauden became the first substitute to be used by Sunderland on September 6th 1965, when he replaced Mike Hellawell at Aston Villa. Hellawell was the last first-class cricketer to play for Sunderland. He'd played for Warwickshire in 1962 and a year later had been capped twice by England at football.

Thirteen home wins cancelled out terrible away form and although 19th place, just three points away from the dreaded drop, was uncomfortable, the table was so tight that Sunderland were only a point behind thirteenth-placed Blackpool.

In the summer of 1966, the World Cup involved four games at Roker Park. In readiness for the competition, the ground underwent several improvements, most notably the roofing of the Fulwell End, which also had temporary benches installed, while new seats were put in the Clock Stand. Group games at Roker saw Italy beat Chile 2-0 then lose 1-0 to the USSR, before the Soviets beat Chile 2-1. Inspired by the great Lev Yashin in goal, the USSR remained at Roker for the quarter final, in which they beat Hungary 2-1, with goals from Chislenko and Porkujan, while Ferenc Bene replied for the Magyars.

Boosted by World Cup success, the domestic game resumed in a buoyant state but unlike most clubs, Sunderland didn't enjoy an attendances boom. Indeed, the average gate dropped by almost three thousand but considering only two of the first twelve games were won, this was hardly surprising. However, home form again kept the club clear of relegation but away from home, results continued to be deplorable. Over the two seasons there were only three away wins compared to twenty eight defeats.

It was just as well that the club was favoured by home draws in the FA Cup. A dozen goals in two games were smashed past lower league Brentford and Peterborough, with Scottish international centre forward, Neil Martin's hat-trick in the 7-1 win over 'The Posh' being only the second post-war FA Cup hat-trick by a Sunderland player.

Martin was on the mark again in the fifth round against Leeds in a 1-1 draw at Roker but the day was marred by injury to teenager, Bobby Kerr. The tiny Scot had made a scoring New Year's Eve debut against Manchester City and had inspired an eleven-game unbeaten run in which he'd scored seven goals, including two in a 3-0 win over Newcastle a week earlier. Six years to the day of that derby, Willie McPheat had scored his dramatic cup goal against Spurs but in the intervening period had broken his leg against Leeds. So when Kerr had his leg broken in a challenge by Norman Hunter, the atmosphere created by the Roker Roar became white hot.

The 1-1 scoreline was repeated in the replay, when boosted by around 20,000 travelling members of the 'Roker Roar', Leeds achieved what is still their record gate. It was into injury time in the second replay at Hull when Leeds were given a controversial, not to say dubious, penalty that resulted in Mulhall and fellow Scottish international, George Herd (a club record signing from Clyde for £38,000 in 1961), being sent off for disputing it. Leeds went through but it only made 1973 even sweeter for Sunderland supporters.

The nucleus of the 1973 cup-winning side was taking shape. Monty was already well established and Bobby Kerr would, of course, re-emerge to lift the cup. He had been a member of Sunderland's losing 1966 FA Youth Cup Final side along with Billy Hughes, who was still in the side when the trophy was won in 1967. Two years later, when the Youth Cup was won again, the team included Ritchie Pitt as a 3-0 first leg deficit was overturned with a 6-0 crushing of West Brom.

For most people, the summer of 1967 was the 'Summer of Love' but for Sunderland it was the summer of being the Vancouver Royal Canadians. That was the name Sunderland played under in a tournament that developed into the North American Soccer League. A dozen games were played between late May and early July against teams from South America and Europe, who all represented U.S. or Canadian cities, Stoke, for instance, being the Cleveland Stokers. A record of three wins, five draws and four defeats left Vancouver Royal Canadians in 5th place but such a position was way beyond Sunderland back in the First Division.

Fifteenth place in 1967-68 equalled their best performance in their four years back in the top flight. In December Baxter left and was replaced by Ian Porterfield but a month later, cup defeat to Second Division Norwich cost McColl his job and saw Alan Brown re-introduced as Sunderland manager. A run of four defeats soon had supporters worried but there only two more in the final twelve games as Sunderland picked up. On the last day of the season, a 2-1 win at Manchester ended United's hopes of the title in the month that they were good enough to become the first English winners of the European Cup.

The season had been another one of struggle, with trips to the capital a source of particular horror. Five were conceded at both Chelsea and Spurs, while West Ham inflicted a joint record defeat of 8-0, with World Cup hero, Geoff Hurst, doubling the tally he got in the World Cup Final. Some people may have thought it was all over – and it was for several Sunderland stalwarts. George Mulhall was one of the scorers at Old Trafford a year earlier but he was given a 'free', as 'Bomber' Brown repeated his previous policy of building a young side and moving on older players. It had been Brown who had worked hard to capture Charlie Hurley's signature in 1957 but in the summer of 1969, Sunderland's most-capped player received a free transfer.

A second relegation followed in 1970. Until 1958, relegation was a thing that happened to other clubs but sadly for all Sunderland supporters, it has become an all-too-frequent experience. A meagre 26 points were the fewest managed since the 1897 flirtation with relegation but a dozen fewer games had been played in Victorian times. No-one was amused! For a club of Sunderland's size to be relegated once was bad enough but to be relegated twice looked like carelessness!

On the night Sunderland went down, Liverpool were the visitors. Managed by the inimitable Bill Shankly, who had been in the Preston side Sunderland had beaten on their only FA Cup win back in 1937, it was strongly rumoured that Liverpool wouldn't have been heartbroken if Sunderland won and stayed up. Hetton-born Bob Paisley was Shankly's assistant manager. Undoubtedly, their celebrations were muted when fullback, Chris Lawler, almost apologetically scored the only goal of the game with four minutes left. Rumours of Liverpool-donated champagne in the Sunderland dressing room resurfaced eleven years later, when a final day win at Anfield produced a more successful escape from the relegation trapdoor.

Relegation in 1970 caused spirits to fall to an all-time low. Anglo Italian games against Lazio and Fiorentina a fortnight after the final league game drew tiny attendances, as supporters showed their displeasure. Playing in those games, when he could have been bound for Mexico, was immaculate defender, Colin Todd. Having been in England's squad of forty for the 1970 World Cup, 'Toddo' missed out on the final party and when he was transferred to Brian Clough's Derby County the following February, it was another blow to supporters who saw him as the new Stan Anderson.

An immediate promotion looked out of the question when seven goals were leaked in the first two games back in the Second Division, even though Sunderland scored just one less in losing 4-3 and drawing 3-3. Former England centre forward, Joe Baker, got among the goals after struggling to find the net in the First Division but he left a month after Dave Watson became Sunderland's first £100,000 signing in December. Scottish Under-23 right back, Dick Malone, had recently joined from Ayr United to replace Cec Irwin, as the lowering of the average age of the team continued.

Having lost badly to Fourth Division Lincoln City in the League Cup despite Monty typically saving a penalty, the FA Cup brought hope of glory, as it had in the previous spell out of the top flight. A third-round tie with Orient saw Sunderland wear all light blue at home because of a rule requiring both sides to change in the event of a colour clash but on a snow-covered pitch there was further despair. Two shots went in off the post in a 3-0 home defeat, at a time when it seemed nothing would go right. Soon afterwards, a run of six games without a goal, followed by another two defeats, resulted in a crowd of less than nine thousand attending a game with Swindon, a surprise 5-2 win that sparked a seven-game unbeaten run, curtailed by a home defeat to Millwall in the last game of the season.

Torrential rain and a crowd of under 10,000 greeted the 1971-72 season, when promising Scottish midfielder, Bobby Park, had his career ended by a broken leg in a 1-1 draw with Birmingham City. Injury had also brought the curtain down on Martin Harvey's career in the spring. Only Charlie Hurley won more caps while on Sunderland's books than Harvey's 34 for Northern Ireland.

Brown's side averaged a point a game away from home in contrast to the largely wretched returns from their travels in recent seasons and a reasonably encouraging fifth place was reached. Although average crowds dipped below 16,000, the missing thousands were evidently ready to come back at the first sign of possible success. An FA Cup replay with Cardiff, for instance, drew over 39,000, despite being played on a

Monday afternoon during the miners' strike, which meant a floodlight ban. A second replay was needed, which Cardiff won at Manchester City's Maine Road.

Had Sunderland won that tie, they would have once again faced Leeds United in the cup. At the end of the season they again dabbled unsuccessfully in the Anglo-Italian tournament, little knowing that, despite the depths the club had sunk to, in a year's time they would have gained access to major European competition after putting one over their old foes from Leeds at Wembley.

MESSIAH, McMENEMY & THE MOVE FROM ROKER (1972-1997).

Sunderland's greatest post-war season began with derby defeat on Teesside and a meagre gate of under 13,000 for the opening home game, which began an encouraging seven-game unbeaten run. However, a sequence of poor results beginning with a 5-1 defeat at Oxford soon followed and with it brought about the departure of manager, Alan Brown. Billy Elliott briefly took over as caretaker boss before the appointment of former Newcastle centre half, Bob Stokoe.

Stokoe's first decision was to revert back from white to black shorts for the first time since 1961. As the team ran out to the tune of 'Z Cars', a rejuvenated Roker Roar greeted the return to tradition. Some supporters had vowed not to return until Alan Brown, who had been in charge of the only two relegations the club had suffered, departed. League leaders, Burnley, were in town for Stokoe's first game, winning on Wearside, as they had in Sunderland's very first league match way back in 1890. But this was a new start for Sunderland. A week later they trailed at Portsmouth with only three minutes to go, only for those stalwart Scots, Hughes and Kerr, to turn defeat into victory and spark the sensational rise of a team who, by the end of the season, were the darlings not only of the nation but of the whole footballing world.

In his first programme notes after becoming manager, Bob Stokoe said, "I am no miracle worker. I make you only one promise: that I shall do absolutely everything in my power to put Sunderland where they belong - right at the top of the tree." Within six months, as Sunderland paraded the FA Cup around Wembley Stadium, Stokoe, who was already known as 'The Messiah', was quoted on the BBC radio commentary insisting, "Until you've seen football in the north east, you've never seen it."

Stokoe strengthened, acquiring Newcastle reserve defenders, Ron Guthrie and David Young, for a combined fee of £35,000. Initially, progress was held up by postponements but when the weather relented, Brighton were beaten 4-0. The following month, the 'house full' signs were up, as over 50,000 piled into Roker. Water into wine, indeed.

In the meantime, 'Boro had got the same 4-0 drubbing as had been handed out to Brighton and after buying Billy Hughes' brother, John, who was badly injured in his only game, Stokoe signed the only other player he brought in to transform a team he had inherited in fourth-bottom place in the Second Division into cup winners. That player was centre forward, Vic Halom - the man for whom cult hero status was invented.

The first 50,000 gate was for the fifth-round replay with Manchester City - a game that was voted Roker's greatest when the ground closed after ninety nine years. Halom scored an absolute blockbuster of a shot from the angle of the penalty area to round off a flowing move and put Sunderland ahead against the cup favourites. It was that night, which saw a brace of goals from Billy Hughes, that convinced all those who had already caught cup fever that Sunderland's name was on the cup.

The cup run began inauspiciously enough at Meadow Lane, where Notts County led 1-0 late in the game, when magnificent Montgomery made a flying save to stop a Les Bradd header strangling Sunderland's cup run at birth. Dave Watson, back at his first club, notched an equaliser and was on the mark again in a comfortable replay win.

Charlie Hurley was manager of Reading, who came to Roker in the fourth round. His goalkeeper, Steve Death, lived up to his name by playing out of his skin to earn Reading a 1-1 draw but rampant Sunderland were two up inside quarter of an hour in the reply at Elm Park and won 3-1.

More than 15,000 Sunderland supporters were in the 54,478 crowd at Maine Road for the fifth round. City took an early lead through Tony Towers, who was later sent off but three years later would help Sunderland to promotion. Going in the opposite direction in due course would be Mickey Horswill. The ginger midfielder played a crucial role in the big cup games, nullifying City's Colin Bell and later, in the semi final and final, he would stop Alan Ball and Johnny Giles from dictating. It was Horswill who got Sunderland back into the game, brilliantly reading a short free kick from City 'keeper, Joe Corrigan, to left back Willie Donachie. Horswill won possession, lifted the ball over Donachie and walloped it past Corrigan.

Midway through the second half, Sunderland stunned City by going ahead. Billy Hughes and Dennis Tueart had devastating pace. Whippets wouldn't take them on and when Tueart put Hughes away, he scorched past the home rearguard to score. City piled on the pressure, forcing Monty into a series of flying saves and got their equaliser when Monty couldn't keep out a corner taken by Mike Summerbee, whose son, Nick, would score for Sunderland at Wembley a generation later. For excitement and drama, the two games with Manchester City had everything.

In the quarter final, Sunderland were drawn at home to Second Division Luton, to whom they had lost a week before the big day. Roared on by another huge crowd, a hard-fought 2-0 win was secured with two goals from second half corners, Watson and Guthrie scoring at the Roker End.

Semi-final opponents, Arsenal, had taken over from Manchester City as cup favourites and were looking to reach their third successive final. Sunderland, though, played exhilarating football and took the lead when the Gunners' centre half, Jeff Blockley's underhit back pass allowed Vic Halom to give Sunderland a first-half lead. Tueart set Hughes up for the second goal, as he had at Manchester City, although this time it was a headed flick on from a long throw that led to Hughes sending a looping header over Arsenal 'keeper, Bob Wilson. With six minutes left, Charlie George pulled a goal back but there was no stopping Sunderland, whose followers wouldn't leave afterwards until Stokoe had returned to the pitch to be saluted.

Sunderland's Wembley side could only muster an England schoolboy appearance by Ritchie Pitt as their Wembley experience. Cup holders, Leeds, who had a European Cup Winners' Cup Final against AC Mllan coming up, were perhaps the hottest favourites ever in the final. However, Sunderland had already seen off two cup favourites and had a smattering of people backing them such as Brian Clough, Bill Shankly and Arsenal 'keeper, Bob Wilson. On Wearside, most supporters were more than optimistic – they were absolutely convinced that Sunderland's name was on the cup and many pointed out that the year of '73 reversed the digits from Sunderland's only previous cup win in '37.

Attempts to give both sides equal tickets proved laughable, as, when the teams emerged, it became apparent that every neutral entitled to a ticket either had Wearside connections or had decided to back the underdogs. The Roker Roar swirled around Wembley and when Ritchie Pitt scythed down England striker, Allan Clarke, in the opening seconds, Leeds realised that Sunderland weren't there to play the role of plucky losers.

Wilson and Montgomery leave the field after the 1973 FA Cup semi final.

Stokoe had already triumphed in the pre-match build up by publicly stating that he hoped the referee and not Leeds skipper, Billy Bremner, would be in charge. Referee Ken Burns, of Stourbridge, duly would have none of Leeds' notorious gamesmanship. Sunderland were a team full of flair. Tueart, Hughes and co. had entertained the nation on TV on the morning of the final with a laughing box during a team interview, while Leeds, by comparison, looked dour and nervous. Stokoe had freed the spirit. Only Guthrie and Halom of 'Stokoe's Stars', as they were known, hadn't been at the club when 'The Messiah' arrived just five months earlier.

Leeds' Scotland winger, Eddie Gray, had been billed in the press as the match winner but it was two of Sunderland's four Scots who marked him out of the game so effectively that he was substituted. Stokoe had detailed 'Captain Kerr' to to 'boldly go' and double up with fullback, Malone.

Sunderland had historically been a club with strong Scottish connections and just past the half-hour mark, the other two Scots shocked the world. After Kerr's hanging lob had been tipped over for a corner at the Sunderland end furthest away from the tunnel, Billy Hughes stepped up to drive across the flag kick. Halom managed to bundle the ball towards Ian Porterfield, who hooked home a right-foot volley from eight yards. As the net bulged, everyone who had watched Monty through the years when it seemed as if he sometimes played teams on his own, knew that the cup was won. Sunderland had done the hard part and scored. Leeds could do what they liked - Monty was going to let no-one beat him now.

Watson, in a 'man of the match' performance, proved he had the ability that would lead to him becoming Sunderland's most capped England international. Horswill patrolled the midfield like an armed vigilante looking for troublemakers and along with Guthrie, seemed determined to score. Sunderland had to give everything and more to retain the lead but in the history of Wembley Stadium, perhaps only Geoff Hurst's World Cup Final goal that, arguably, didn't cross the line, has been talked about more than the moment when Montgomery saved from Lorimer.

Twenty minutes were left as Leeds piled on the pressure. Monty dived full length to beat out a far-post diving header from Trevor Cherry, providing easy pickings for Lorimer. Known to have the hardest shot in football, Lorimer had the goal at his mercy from close range and duly 'scored' - only, he didn't, despite the TV commentators saying he had!

From nowhere, Monty had pushed himself up and made the most miraculous save. Leeds now knew what Sunderland had known when the completely left-footed Porterfield scored with his right - it wasn't to be their day. "Easy, Easy," the Sunderland fans taunted Leeds in the closing stages and when the whistle blew and the red tracksuited Stokoe ran to raise Monty high, the world wanted to be a part of Sunderland. "You've never seen scenes like this," the BBC radio commentator informed listeners around the world as the party began on the club's happiest day ever. The day had begun with rain, as coaches and trains emptied at King's Cross in the early hours but the cup glinted in the sunshine on the lap of honour, as the sun came out on Sunderland.

Copies of the 'Football Echo' were flown to London. The pink paper had turned white and then blue with shock when Sunderland were relegated in 1958 but it returned to its original colour in celebration. Back on Wearside, where virtually every house and shop had been decked in red and white for weeks, the people poured onto the streets as tears of joy flowed.

1973 Cup Final managers, Bob Stokoe and Don Revie, had played against each other in the 1955 final, when Stokoe was centre half for Newcastle and Revie, centre forward for Manchester City.

The homecoming was delayed by a league fixture at Cardiff, who got the point they wanted to stay up. Sunderland's own relegation worries had been long banished as they went from strength to strength, moving up to sixth place.

Around a million people lined the thirteen-mile route from Carrville, in Durham, to Roker Park when the cup came home on the Tuesday night. Every vantage point was taken. Supporters carried a coffin marked 'Leeds Utd R.I.P'. around Roker Park before 'The Lads' came out to take their bow.

Twenty-four hours later, promoted QPR turned up and beat Sunderland 3-0. Goalkeeper, Phil Parkes, was inspired and when QPR's Stan Bowles deliberately kicked the ball out to knock the FA Cup off its table on the halfway line, the mood turned ugly. Severely unimpressed with the referee, who never took another Sunderland game, one fan (wrongly) came onto the pitch to chase the official with a corner flag and had to be restrained by Sunderland players.

Bob Stokoe celebrates the famous FA Cup victory against Leeds, 1973.

Expectations were, of course, now high. A low-key 3-0 friendly defeat at Aberdeen began the 1973-74 season for the cup holders but this was followed by a 2-1 win at Celtic, who had been champions of Scotland for eight years running. Sunderland paraded the cup at Parkhead before the game and played as if they would go on to walk the Second Division.

However, it was soon discovered that, now Sunderland had been in a cup final they had forty-two more to contend with, as every club saw their fixtures with Sunderland as their matches of the season. Half a dozen games into the campaign, Pitt received a career-ending injury. The only promotion issue at the end of the season was that a late fightback ended visitors, Blackpool's promotion chances at Roker and four days later, a 4-3 win at promoted Luton raised hopes that sixth-placed Sunderland would go up next time.

For the first time, Sunderland had had to contend with three major cup competitions. The defence of the FA Cup had ended tamely in a 1-0 home third-round replay defeat against Carlisle, while the League Cup provided plenty of excitement. A thrilling three-match encounter with high-flying Derby started with a great 2-2 draw at The Baseball Ground and a wonderful replay that ended 1-1, with 'man of the match', Tueart, having a penalty brilliantly saved. Two nights later, Vic Halom scored a sensational hat-trick against Roy McFarland, the centre half hitherto keeping Watson out of the England team, as Sunderland won the second replay 3-0.

Sunderland hadn't taken their place in the pre-season Wembley Charity Shield, preferring to entertain League Cup holders, Spurs, so when champions, Liverpool, arrived for the next round of the League Cup, the traditional Charity Shield contestants finally got to meet. It was Liverpool who won 2-0, with two fortunate goals, a fortnight after Sunderland's European interest had ended.

The Cup Winners' Cup adventure began against Vasas, in Budapest, where Tueart ran half the length of the pitch to score a great goal, which, combined with a Hughes header, provided a handsome 2-0 win. The crowd for the return leg was kept down to 22,762 by the doubling of admission charges to see a Tueart penalty ensure a 3-0 aggregate victory.

Goals from Kerr and Horswill looked to have earned a comfortable cushion to take to Sporting Lisbon in the next round, only for Hector Yazalde, who won the 'Golden Boot' as Europe's top scorer that year, to net a valuable late away goal. Sunderland went down 2-0 in Lisbon, where the ball boys quickly disappeared after not-so-Sporting went ahead on aggregate. UEFA fined them later but Sunderland's European dreams were over for an awfully long time.

The cup-winning team started to break up, Tueart and Horswill going to Manchester City in March, with Towers coming to Roker in part-exchange. Watson would follow them to Maine Road at the end of the next season.

Freed from the tag of being cup holders, the 1974-75 campaign got off to a bright start. Four wins in the first five games encouraged hopes for a side strengthened by the introduction of former Scotland and Newcastle captain Bobby Moncur and Sunderland-born Pop Robson, who two years earlier had been the First Division's leading scorer with

West Ham. Moncur coming to Roker was likened to Anderson going to St James in 1963 and this comparison became stronger when the Scot marshalled the side towards promotion.

Only one of the first thirteen games was lost, as Sunderland became embroiled in a four-horse race for three promotion positions. Manchester United were on their way straight back up after relegation and took an early lead against Sunderland at Old Trafford before over 60,000 in a match voted BBC's 'Match of the Season'. "Oh, how'd you win the cup?" teased the Stretford End, before two quick goals from Billy Hughes silenced them as the Wearside fans replied, "That's how we won the cup." United won the game 3-2 but much worse was a serious car crash to Ian Porterfield a week later. The cup final scorer played brilliantly in a 4-1 home win over Portsmouth the day before his accident, which ruled him out for the rest of the season. He did make a comeback before leaving for Sheffield Wednesday in 1977 and later embarked on a managerial career that included Rotherham (where he was joined by Vic Halom), Sheffield United, Aberdeen (where he succeeded Alex Ferguson) and Chelsea, before going into international management in Africa.

Only three thousand less than had been at Old Trafford turned up for the last game of the season at Villa Park, including many thousands from Sunderland. Villa ended Sunderland's promotion hopes with a 2-0 win and went up with Man Utd and Norwich, whom they beat 4-1 at Carrow Road four days later.

There were to be no mistakes when promotion was finally achieved in 1975-76. Jeff Clarke replaced Watson in central defence and Joe Bolton took over at left back from Ron Guthrie. Fantastic home form was the key to success. Despite ten away defeats, the Second Division Championship was won thanks to a record of nineteen wins from twenty-one home games. Only the two Bristol clubs left Roker with a point.

Thoughts of another cup win began to surface when Third Division Crystal Palace were drawn at Roker in the quarter final. Fedora-wearing Palace manager, Malcolm Allison, had been with Manchester City in the cup classic three years earlier but this time he left smiling after seeing Alan Whittle give his side a surprise victory in a scrappy game.

The first aim, though, was always promotion and this was sealed with a 2-1 Easter Monday win against a Bolton side that included Sam Allardyce and Barry Siddall, who would later play at Sunderland, as well as Peter Reid, who would later become manager. The first of those to arrive was goalkeeper, Siddall, who took over from Montgomery. Monty's record 623rd and last match was at Old Trafford in the League Cup, the same competition in which he had made his debut in 1961. Montgomery was only thirty-three, an age at which goalkeepers are now thought to be approaching their peak. He later returned to Sunderland as a reserve 'keeper but wasn't called upon at first-team level. In the 1980s and '90s he had two spells coaching the club's youth teams and had a suite named after him at Roker Park.

Siddall joined record signing, Bob Lee, the club's first £200,000 player. A centre forward, Lee had the physique but was constantly handicapped by a rumour that Sunderland had gone to his club, Leicester, aiming to sign England forward, Frank Worthington but got Lee instead. Worthington eventually had a brief spell at Sunderland five years later.

Lee took criticism when bottom-of-the-table Sunderland went a record ten league games without a goal. The town's motto, 'Nil Desperandum', took on new meaning for the thousands looking at it on Wearmouth Bridge as they crossed it heading to Roker Park.

In later years, Bob Stokoe expressed his regret at resigning just nine games into the season and after a spell under caretaker Ian MacFarlane, Jimmy Adamson took over the reins. It was under Adamson that the goals dried up. Adamson had played under Alan Brown at Burnley and had managed the Turf Moor outfit the previous season, when they had gone down.

Like his mentor, Adamson turned to youth. Gary Rowell had broken into the team in the promotion year and he was soon joined by Kevin Arnott and Shaun Elliott. This talented trio brought new hope. Rowell went on to beat Shackleton's post-war scoring record, Elliott won an England 'B' cap at Roker within three years and was robbed of captaining Sunderland at Wembley in 1985 through suspension, while Arnott could and should have become a great player, with his passing ability but grew too fond of preferring to occupy the centre circle rather than the whole pitch. Given Bobby Kerr's engine, Arnott would have been world-class. Another of Adamson's youngsters was speed merchant striker, Alan Brown (no relation). He did everything but score when he came into the team, hitting the bar at Highbury and Anfield as the goal drought persisted.

Eventually, after points from successive goalless draws ended a run of nine defeats, the duck was broken by the late Mel Holden, as Bristol City went down 1-0 in a rare Friday night fixture at Roker. Suddenly every shot was going in! Middlesbrough were trounced 4-0, Lee got a hat-trick as West Brom were thrashed 6-1 and West Ham were walloped 6-0.

The run ended before a huge midweek following at Manchester City, where a dubious penalty converted by Dennis Tueart and an outrageous decision to disallow a Holden 'goal' for offside when he was behind the ball, combined to make people think Sunderland were destined for the drop, after all.

Nonetheless, the side continued to pick up points and with Adamson rallying support, a nine-match unbeaten run was protected in the penultimate game when little Bobby Kerr left the bench to score, as two late goals from the 'Black Cat' club clawed a point from the 'Canaries' at Carrow Road.

The 'Russian roulette' of relegation came down to a shoot out that was meant to be simultaneous. One of Sunderland, Coventry or Bristol City would go down with Spurs and Stoke. Sunderland kicked off their Thursday night match at Everton on time and lost 2-0. Coventry and Bristol City faced each other at Highfield Road, where the losers would go down but a draw would keep both up if Sunderland lost. Rumours that Coventry were leading 3-1 spread around the red and white legions in the 36,000 crowd at Goodison but the truth was that Coventry's game had kicked off late. Once Sunderland's final score was flashed onto the Highfield Road scoreboard, the two sides played out a farcical finale with all the competitive edge of a pre-season friendly, no-one taking a shot as both sides ensured their joint safety.

Coventry's delay was said to be due to the size of the gate but there were 36,000 at both games, yet only one kicked off on time. Coventry were later reprimanded by the Football League but it did Sunderland as much good as the slap to Sporting Lisbon three seasons earlier. In 1997, when Sunderland were again relegated, away to Wimbledon, history repeated itself, when across London, rivals, Coventry's match at Spurs started late, allowing them to know exactly what was required to stay up.

Despite a dismal 3-0 defeat at Hull in the first match back in the Second Division, over 31,000 turned up for the first home game, hoping to see 'The Lads' make their stay in the second tier as short as it had been at the top. Though Burnley were beaten 3-0, a head start was given to the rest of the division when Sunderland took until mid-October to win again and though things picked up, with leading scorer, Rowell, netting nineteen, the club finished sixth in the Second Division for the third time in six years.

Adamson didn't last much longer. Supporters were generally pleased when Leeds asked him to succeed Jock Stein in November 1978. His assistant, Dave Merrington, had a spell in charge before Billy Elliott took over for the second half of the season.

Elliott got the side playing good football. Clarke and Elliott had formed an excellent central defensive partnership, ex-England fullback, Steve Whitworth, was brought in and was consistent but never popular, while hard man, Joe Bolton, operated at left back.

Mick Docherty (son of Tommy) was one of a number of ex-Burnley players who had arrived during Adamson's tenure and he anchored the midfield, while up front, penalty king, Rowell, became the first striker to manage twenty league goals since Neil Martin. His haul included an heroic hat-trick in a 4-1 win at Newcastle but he was badly injured soon after and missed the last ten fixtures.

Losing two of the last three home games either side of a thrilling 6-2 home win over Sheffield Utd proved costly. Promotion depended on winning the last game of the season at Wrexham and needing other results to go well. Predictably, thousands upon thousands travelled to Wales but although Sunderland won, as in 1958 and 1977, results elsewhere didn't go as hoped and Sunderland missed out.

Elliott had done well but was replaced by Ken Knighton for the Centenary season. Charlie Hurley was voted 'Player of the Century' by supporters and an England XI beat Sunderland 2-0 at Roker, with two goals from Bob Latchford, in the Centenary game. The Centenary celebration everyone wanted, though, was promotion and Knighton delivered it, using the 1976 recipe of strong home form.

Ten of eleven games before Christmas were won and the unbeaten home league record was protected all season. Crowds meant money and Knighton broke the club transfer record twice in the month before Christmas, bringing in midget, Stan Cummins, from Middlesbrough for £300,000 and Argentinian, Claudio Marangoni, for £320,000.

Cummins was a hit. His wing play was allied with a dozen goals, including four against Burnley, one against Newcastle on the last occasion Sunderland would win a Tyne-Wear derby at Roker and a brilliant shot on the night promotion was won. West Ham were the visitors, just two days after beating Arsenal in the FA Cup Final. The gates were locked with just over 47,000 in the ground to see Arnott complement Cummins' strike in a 2-0 win.

Cummins would also score on the final day of the 1980-81 season. His Anfield winner helped keep Sunderland up, although, for once, other results had helped anyway. Sunderland had briefly topped the embryonic table after winning the two opening games, with John Hawley hitting a hat-trick at Manchester City. Marangoni never settled and returned to South America, where he later became South American 'Player of the Year'.

Tom Cowie had taken over from Keith Collings as Chairman. Apart from a three-year spell under Jack Parker between 1968 and 1971, the Collings family, in the shape of Keith and his father, Syd, had been in the Chair since 1960. When shirt sponsorship came in, Cowies were the first sponsors until brewers, Vaux, began their long-term commitment. After the closure of Vaux in 1999, Reg Vardy Garages took over.

Cowie had given Knighton and his assistant, Frank Clark, the push, leaving Mick Docherty to guide Sunderland through the final four fixtures. Alan Durban was appointed as Sunderland's first Welsh manager and he built a side that, in later years, supporters accepted was potentially the best Sunderland had had since the cup-winning team.

Considering the furore over the move from black to white shorts in 1961 criticism was muted when Sunderland ditched their traditional kit for a set of pyjamas in 1981. The le Coq Sportif kit consisted of a white shirt with very thin stripes set widely apart with red shorts and socks. The strip lasted for two years before a more traditional kit returned.

Durban signed a little-known striker from St Johnstone and a hard man in Scottish international defender, Iain Munro. The striker was Ally McCoist. He scored only eight goals in 56 appearances, a third of which were as a substitute, before he was offloaded to Rangers, where he became their greatest ever scorer. Nearly two decades later, when scouting for Sunderland, it was Durban who spotted and recommended Kevin Phillips. Durban's two full seasons brought finishes of 19th and 16th but he was building a side, developing England Under-21 fullbacks, Barry Venison and Nick Pickering, while adding experience in the form of Frank Worthington and Welsh winger, Leighton James.

Team-building continued into 1983-84. A new midfield pairing of Paul Bracewell and Mark Proctor was brought in, soon to be followed by striker Lee Chapman. Good away form that included wins at Highbury and Anfield came unstuck in a 6-1 defeat at Notts County. The turn of the year, though, brought a run of seven league games without a win, combined with a disappointing home cup exit, so it was no great surprise when Durban was sacked. After Pop Robson stood in as manager for a home draw with Arsenal, Sunderland turned to one of their most loyal servants in Len Ashurst to be the new manager.

No outfield player has played more games for Sunderland than 'Lenny the Lion.' A player between 1957 and 1971, the Liverpudlian had had a testimonial against Newcastle and been an ever-present in the 1964 promotion team. Ashurst brought in a clutch of new signings, most notably Gary Bennett, who he had managed at Cardiff. By the end of Benno's time at Roker, only Stan Anderson could join Ashurst and claim to have played more games for Sunderland as an outfield player than Bennett.

Although not Sunderland's first black player - that was Roly Gregoire in 1978 - Bennett's contribution to the club did an enormous amount to significantly reduce, if not totally remove, the scourge of racism from the terraces.

Under Ashurst, Sunderland initially staved off the threat of relegation in 1984, attained the dizzy heights of seventh in the First Division in November and reached Wembley in the League (Milk) Cup Final. The ten-game cup run was inspired by brilliant goalkeeper, Chris Turner, who had been at the club since 1979 and had displaced Siddall.

Striker, Colin West, had scored three times in the two-leg semi with Chelsea, Sunderland winning 2-0 at home and 3-2 in London, where West almost had to dodge a police horse to score. It wasn't that Chelsea were fielding donkeys but not impressed at being beaten, the home fans rioted with some coming onto the pitch. If they thought it was all over, it soon was for Ashurst.

He controversially left West out at Wembley, where Sunderland failed miserably. Clive Walker missed a penalty and the only goal of the game was deflected into his own net by Gordon Chisholm after the inexperienced David Corner was robbed on the goal line.

Not unusually, the only saving grace Sunderland could point to was their supporters. Following recent riots, including the behaviour of Chelsea's fans in the semi, they drew praise for their sporting reaction to defeat in what became known as the 'Friendly Final'. Seven years later, when Norwich were beaten by Sunderland in the semi final of the FA Cup, their followers responded with equal grace. Not one of the remaining dozen league games was won and in eight of them, Sunderland failed to score. Relegation was inevitable and they were joined by their Wembley conquerors, Norwich.

If it had been a bad season there was worse, much worse to follow. At the time, the appointment of Lawrie McMenemy was hailed as a great move, with Sunderland at last thinking big again. McMenemy had won the cup with Southampton but as far as the supporters were concerned, his time at Sunderland was the biggest disaster since the Titanic left the same town.

McMenemy's policy was to bring in star names who were in the twilight of their careers. Some came good, Eric Gates and Frank Gray, for instance but results were terrible. In his first game, Blackburn, managed by Bobby Saxton, who would later coach Sunderland under Peter Reid, gave a footballing lesson at Roker. The first five games were lost without a goal being scored and by the end of the season, the final two games had to be won to avoid the unthinkable drop into Division Three.

On loan goalkeeper, Andy 'Officer' Dibble, had done well in in his ten games and two vital clean sheets helped towards 2-0 wins over Shrewsbury and Stoke. McMenemy waved a white handkerchief at the crowd, as hopes were rekindled that a fresh start would see an improvement.

Basically, though, Sunderland had seen the iceberg and continued full steam towards it. A first-day 2-0 win at Mick Buxton's Huddersfield raised hopes but if anyone thought it was an omen, as the club's first promotion had started with an identical win on the same ground, then they were in for a shock. There would be a first at the end of the season but it was a first trip into the lower reaches of the league!

The next away game brought a 6-1 defeat at Blackburn. Defeat at Sheffield United started a seven-game run without a win but it was when the 'Blades' cut Sunderland down before only 8,544 at Roker in April that McMenemy left. Angry crowds gathered at the main entrance to the ground afterwards, demanding his dismissal. If Sunderland were the Titanic, the ex-Guardsman sneaked onto his own lifeboat and made his escape. McMenemy had been on an astronomical salary and had a house with everything paid for. He disappeared in the middle of the night and was long gone when his departure was announced.

Needing a miracle, new Chairman, Bob Murray, brought in Bob Stokoe. Unlucky to lose 3-2 at Bradford in his first match, he witnessed goalkeeper, Iain Hesford, who had had a nightmare season, concede a goal from forty yards on his return to Roker, for a 1-1 draw with Leeds, of all teams. Bennett got a winner at Shrewsbury before Bradford repeated their 3-2 win at Roker. Youngster, Gordon Armstrong, scored in a 1-0 win and a 1-1 draw, before the last game of the season left Sunderland needing a home win against Barnsley to stay up.

Proctor missed a penalty as Barnsley came from behind to win and condemn Sunderland to a two-leg Play-Off with Gillingham of the Third Division, with a Play-Off Final to follow for the winners. Not since the 'Test Matches' of 1897 had Sunderland faced such a situation. The first leg was lost 3-2 in Kent, where Tony Cascarino scored a hat-trick. Gillingham went further ahead with an early goal at Roker and in a dramatic match in which Gates scored twice, both sides missed penalties before Gary Bennett took the match into extra time with a majestic Fulwell End header in the dying minutes. The 3-2 Roker scoreline meant that, in extra time, a further goal each would send Sunderland down, as away goals counted double and Gillingham had an extra half-hour to take advantage.

Cascarino quickly scored again to take his tally to five in the two games and Sunderland slipped quietly into the Third Division, having only been able to muster a diving header by Keith Bertschin, which won the game but not the tie. Newcastle supporters in the Clock Stand Paddock celebrated Sunderland's relegation but the next time Sunderland featured in a Play-Off tie it would be Newcastle's turn to suffer.

Goal average cost Sunderland their first relegation in 1958 and in 1987, when they dropped into the Third Division, it was the away goals rule that sunk the final nail into the coffin.

Denis Smith was appointed as Sunderland's eleventh post-war manager. The former Stoke centre half had done well as manager at York, who wanted £10,000 compensation. Smith stated that if Sunderland didn't gain immediate promotion, he'd pay it out of his own pocket. By his own admission, Smith was arrogant but his achievement in taking Sunderland straight back up shouldn't be underestimated. Other big clubs have sunk into the Third Division and struggled. Some, such as Wolves at this time, for instance, were in Division Four!

Sunderland travelled to Brentford - the scene of the club's first League Cup tie - for their opening game in Division Three, where Bertschin got them off to a winning start. Smith had brought in defenders John Kay and John MacPhail cheaply and soon bought again, bringing young striker, Marco Gabbiadini, from his former club. There was a parallel with Bob Stokoe's seventies signings of Guthrie and Young, followed by Halom. Kay and MacPhail tightened the defence, MacPhail also proving to be a penalty kick specialist, while Gabbiadini, like Halom, quickly became a hero.

Having hit the post on his debut, Marco scored twice in each of his next three games. He struck up a fantastic understanding with the veteran, Gates, who consistently gave Gabbiadini the ball where he wanted it. The 'G Force' both topped twenty goals for the season. Sunderland, who hadn't scored seven in a game for twenty years, suddenly did so twice in three weeks. Gates sealed promotion at Port Vale, the Championship was clinched at home to Northampton and the party took place at Rotherham, where thousands turned up in fancy dress to say goodbye to the Third Division, as a 4-1 win condemned Rotherham to the relegation Play Offs.

Smith and his assistant, Viv Busby, consolidated Sunderland's place in the Second Division, 11th place representing a rare year without end-of-season nerves at either end of the table for Sunderland supporters. Apart from 1984, when 13th place still involved having to win away to Leicester in the final game to be sure of avoiding relegation, Sunderland hadn't had a mid table placing since 1971.

The 1989-90 season began and ended with games against Swindon Town. A 2-0 first day win in Wiltshire provided encouragement and set the standard for impressive away performances that saw Sunderland reach double figures in away wins for the first time ever in the Second Division.

Sixth place gave entry to the Play-Offs and a two-leg meeting with local rivals, Newcastle United. The 'Magpies' came to Roker first and fought out a typically dour goalless draw. In the last minute, Newcastle were outraged when Sunderland were awarded a penalty for a Mark Stimson foul on Gabbiadini in front of a howling Fulwell End. Left back, Paul Hardyman, who had come from Portsmouth, had a good record from the spot but reacted in horror when he saw Burridge save it and was sent off for following up.

With their good away record, Sunderland fancied their chances at St James, where Newcastle felt they were favourites. Gates gave Sunderland an early lead, after which, try as Newcastle might, they couldn't unnerve a composed Sunderland. With four minutes left, Gates and Gabbiadini combined for Marco to make it 2-0 in front of wildly ecstatic Sunderland fans, who enjoyed their best night since the 1973 FA Cup Final. Newcastle's distraught followers invaded the pitch, aiming for an abandonment, forcing World Cup referee, George Courtney, to take the teams off the pitch. Courtney informed everyone that he was going to finish the match if it took him until midnight or beyond. When the teams returned, the main objective seemed to be staying near the tunnel, ready for a quick escape when the final whistle sounded.

Wembley in the Play-Off Final meant a meeting with Swindon, whose fluent football under Ossie Ardiles gave them victory. Goalkeeper, Tony Norman, had been a record signing from Hull eighteen months earlier and he alone stood between Sunderland and a heavy defeat. Only a shot deflected by Gary Bennett conquered Norman but as Wembley emptied, another Second Division season was in prospect.

However, Swindon were subject to an investigation for financial irregularities and when found guilty during the summer, were punished by not only being denied promotion but also being relegated to Division Three. On appeal, that blow was withdrawn and they were allowed to carry on in Division Two but it left a huge debate over who should take the vacant spot in the top flight. Relegated Sheffield Wednesday, who had finished third-bottom stated their case strongly, as did Newcastle, who felt that, as the third-top team in the Second Division, they should go up. It was Sunderland, though, who, as Play-Off Finalists, benefited and found themselves promoted.

Gates and MacPhail were replaced by new signings, Kevin Ball and Peter Davenport. First-day defeat at Norwich was compensated for by an exciting, if goalless, draw with Spurs and a Bennett last-minute winner against Manchester United but there were only two more wins by the turn of the year as relegation loomed.

For the final game at Manchester City, Sunderland had a chance of staying up and roared on by another mass exodus from Wearside, they led 2-1 at one stage, only to slide straight back down as Peter Reid's City side won with two goals from Niall Quinn.

Sunderland struggled badly in the early nineties. Denis Smith was sacked midway through the campaign, with former youth coach, Malcolm Crosby put in temporary charge. The likeable, Sunderland-born Crosby sparked a cup run that resulted in him being given the manager's job, despite a miserable 18th place in the league.

The cup run began with a comfortable home win over Port Vale, followed by victory at Oxford, before the dullest of goalless draws with West Ham on a wind-spoilt Roker day. A brilliant performance by Norman in the replay helped Sunderland to a 3-2 win, with two-goal John Byrne maintaining his record of scoring in every round.

Byrne got a late equaliser at Chelsea in a quarter final played on a Monday night to suit TV requirements, as the modern influence of the media started to bite into football traditions. The tradition of the cup was alive and well in the replay, when, after more heroics from Norman, Chelsea forced a late equaliser and looked strong enough to win in extra time. The last minute of the match, though, produced a moment to rival the ecstasy of the 1973 run. Gordon Armstrong rose, Hurley-like, to power in a header from a corner and put the Second Division strugglers into the semi final. Byrne got the only goal of the game against Norwich at Hillsborough to set up a Wembley meeting with Liverpool.

An even first half saw Byrne fluff a great chance to put Sunderland ahead and become only the tenth man ever to score in every round, while a shot from skipper, Bracewell, in his second spell at the club, took a deflection and drifted inches wide, with 'keeper, Grobbelaar, beaten. Once

Michael Thomas gave Liverpool the lead two minutes after the re-start, though, the second half developed into a one-sided affair, Ian Rush making the final score 2-0 with a goal that made him the leading FA Cup Final scorer of all time.

Losing to Liverpool didn't come as a surprise but there was a shock in the summer, when out-of-contract captain, Paul Bracewell, signed for Newcastle. He went on to lead the 'Magpies' to promotion, while Sunderland continued to struggle badly.

Amongst the new signings when Sunderland reported back for training, was ex-England centre half, Terry Butcher, who had managerial experience with Coventry. His seventy-seven caps made him the most capped player to appear for Sunderland.

With the restructuring of English football and the creation of the Premier League, Sunderland began the 1992-93 season competing for the Football League Championship trophy but not competing against the elite sides. It was probably just as well, as Sunderland found it tough enough in the new First Division. A 6-0 defeat at West Ham was bad enough but when a 5-2 defeat at Peterborough followed soon afterwards, it illustrated how far the club was slipping. On the last day of the season, they could easily have been relegated to the new Second Division and only results elsewhere saved them, as Sunderland slumped to a 3-1 defeat at Notts County.

Butcher had taken over following Crosby's February sacking and in spending over £2m in the summer of 1993, he disposed of more cash than any previous Sunderland manager. He wasn't helped by a pre-season car crash involving several of his new signings and when the season began with a record 5-0 opening day defeat at Derby, the signs looked ominous.

An Autumn run of six successive defeats signalled Butcher's sacking, which was the last act of Bob Murray as Chairman, as he decided to step down but remained on the board, with John Featherstone taking over as figurehead. Murray would resume as Chairman in the summer of 1996.

As with the managerial appointments of Butcher and Crosby, the club decided to promote from within and consequently, coach and former Sunderland boys player, Mick Buxton, took over. Results picked up enough for a mid-table position to at least offer some hope along with the signing of Polish international fullback, Dariusz Kubicki, from Aston Villa.

The longest unbeaten start to a season since 1910 offered encouragement at the start of 1994-95 but only two of the eight unbeaten matches were won and from the beginning of November onwards, Sunderland were never in the top half of the table. With the side hovering dangerously near the relegation zone they had become used to, it was decided to sack Buxton after a particularly poor performance in a Friday night defeat at Barnsley.

Out of the blue, Bob Murray produced former Manchester City manager, Peter Reid, with seven games left. Reid saw Craig Russell score a crucial final minute winner in his first game in charge and Sunderland went on to avoid relegation with the luxury of a game to spare.

Appointed full time, Reid brought his old Everton colleague, Paul Bracewell, back for a third spell at Sunderland, this time as player/assistant manager.

Reid had nothing like the money invested by Terry Butcher three years earlier, Bracewell at £50,000 and John Mullin, a youngster from Burnley, costing an initial £40,000, being the newcomers. A home defeat on the first day of the season, followed by a struggle to knock lower league Preston out of the League Cup, didn't augur well and a month into the season, Sunderland were languishing in 15th place.

A scrambled home win over bogey team, Southend, started an eleven game unbeaten run in the league, with a couple of cup performances against Liverpool a sign of things to come, as Reid got his team organised and developed a passing game. A steady rise up the table climaxed with an explosive 6-0 slaughter of leaders, Millwall, in December, with Sunderland replacing them on top of the table.

Manchester United were given a run for their money in two FA Cup games not settled until the last minute of the replay and although Sunderland had slipped to seventh by the time goalkeeper Shay Given (one of four loan players used by Reid) made his debut in mid-January, there was a growing belief that Sunderland could go up.

Given kept a remarkable nine clean sheets in his first eleven games, the last of which was a 'match of the season' performance as main rivals Derby were swept aside 3-0 at Roker. That victory was in the middle of a record run of nine successive wins, which left Sunderland in pole position that they weren't to relinquish. The dependable Alec Chamberlain returned in place of the injured Given for the last few games, as the Championship trophy was won sixty years after Raich Carter and co. had last claimed it.

Sunderland's first season in the Premiership was begun in the knowledge that it would be the last at Roker Park, by now in its 99th year. Driven by Bob Murray, a new state-of-the-art stadium was rising on the site of the former Wearmouth Colliery on the banks of the Wear. Previous plans for a stadium in Washington had had to be abandoned following objections from businesses in the area.

Failing to score in four of the opening six fixtures, after ending the Championship season by scoring in only one of the last six games, showed where Sunderland's problems were going to lie. In the club's 117-year history, the lowest top-scoring player had managed seven goals – and that in the 1970 relegation season. However, no player would score more than four all season, as Sunderland fought unsuccessfully to avoid relegation.

Former England internationals, Paul Stewart and Chris Waddle, scored in Roker Park's final league game, with new signing, Allan Johnston, claiming the last ever league goal in a 3-0 win over Everton. However, final day defeat away to Wimbledon condemned the club to the drop for the seventh time.

Just two days later, the fans packed Roker one last time for a farewell match against the stadium's first visitors, Liverpool.

At one time, Roker Park could have fitted what was now its capacity of 22,657 into the Roker End alone. It was a sign of how far the ground had declined. While many other grounds had been redeveloped, Roker Park was largely unchanged from the time it was a World Cup venue in 1966. The 'Farewell to Roker' night caused many to shed a tear. People who had made Roker and Sunderland great paraded around the pitch. Billy Bingham, George Aitken, Chris Turner, Monty, Bob Stokoe, Bobby Kerr (carrying the FA Cup) and Gary Rowell were just a few. Even the grandson of 1890s goalkeeper, Ted Doig, paraded a photograph of his grandad around the pitch.

John Mullin earned the distinction of being the ground's last goalscorer, as the 1-0 scoreline of the very first match was repeated. After the game, Charlie Hurley made a speech from the centre circle before digging up the centre spot to be transported to the club's new home. Many in the crowd didn't want to leave and stayed long, long after the final whistle, chanting 'Red Army' one last time into the darkness.

A month later, the contents of the ground were auctioned off before the diggers moved in to demolish the stadium in preparation for the housebuilders. The demolition of Roker Park was like a bereavement to Sunderland supporters but with the opening of the Stadium of Light, they have seen that the club has been re-born.

The final programme at Roker Park.

HONOURS AND RECORDS

FORMED: 1879

PREVIOUS GROUNDS:

Blue House Field, Hendon 1879-82

The Cedars, 1882

Groves Field, Ashbrooke, 1882-83

Horatio Street, 1883-84

Abbs Field, Fulwell, 1884-86

Newcastle Road, 1886-98

Roker Park 1898 - 1997

FOOTBALL / PREMIER LEAGUE RECORD

Elected to Football League 1890

Stayed in Division One until 1958, holding the record as the only club until then never to play outside the top flight.

Div 2 1958-64

Div 1 1964-70

Div 2 1970-76

Div 1 1976-77

Div 2 1977-80

Div 1 1980-85

Div 2 1985-87

Div 3 1987-88

Div 2 1988-90

Div 1 1990-91

Div 2 1991-92

New Div 1 1992-96

Premier League 1996-97

New Div 1 1997-99

Premier League 1999

MANAGERS:

Tom Watson 1889-96

Robert Campbell 1896-99

Alex Mackie 1899-1905

Robert Kyle 1905-28

Johnny Cochrane 1928-39

Bill Murray 1939-57

Alan Brown 1957-64

George Hardwick 1964-65

Ian McColl 1965-68

Alan Brown 1968-72

Bob Stokoe 1972-76

Ian MacFarlane 1976 (Caretaker)

Jimmy Adamson 1976-78

Dave Merrington 1978 (Caretaker)

Billy Elliott 1978-79

Ken Knighton 1979-81

Mick Docherty 1981 (Caretaker)

Alan Durban 1981-84

Bryan Robson 1984 (Caretaker)

Len Ashurst 1984-85

Lawrie McMenemy 1985-87

Bob Stokoe 1987 (Caretaker)

Denis Smith 1987-91

Malcolm Crosby 1991-93

Terry Butcher 1993-94

Mick Buxton 1994-95

Peter Reid-1995.

HONOURS

Football League Div 1 Champions:

1891-92, 1892-93,1894-95,1901-02,1912-13 & 1935-36

Football League Div 1 Runners-up:

1893-94, 1897-98, 1900-01, 1922-23 & 1934-35

New Div 1 Champions: 1995-96 and 1998-99

Div 2 Champions: 1975-76

Div 2 Runners-up:

1963-64

Promoted from Div 2:

1989-90

Div 3 Champions: 1987-88

FA Cup Winners: 1937 and 1973

FA Cup Runners-up: 1913 and 1992

Football League Cup Runners-up: 1985

FA Charity Shield: Winners 1936, Runners-up 1937

STADIUM STATISTICS

Stadium of Light Capacity: 42,000 (Possibly rising to 63,000)

Record Attendance: 41,680 v Arsenal, 14/9/99, FA Carling Premiership

Roker Park Record Attendance: 75,118 V Derby County,

FA Cup 6th Rd Replay, 8/3/33.

MOST CAPPED PLAYERS

England : Dave Watson (14)

Scotland: Jim Baxter (10)

Wales: Andy Melville (17)

Northern Ireland: Martin Harvey (34)

Republic of Ireland: Charlie Hurley (40)

Appearances & Goals Records:

Most league appearances: Jimmy Montgomery 537 (623 in total)

Most league goals in a season by an individual: Dave Halliday (43, 1928-29)

Most goals by an individual - total: Bobby Gurney (228)

Most league goals by an individual - total: Charlie Buchan (209)

Most post-war goals (All Competitions): Gary Rowel (102)

Record Victories:

League: 5/12/1908, 9-1, away to Newcastle. Joint record First Division away win.

FA Cup: 2/2/1895, 11-1, 1st Rd v Fairfield (H)

League Cup: 9/10/1990, 6-1, 2nd Rd 2nd leg, Bristol City (A)

Record Defeats:

League: 0-8 v Sheff Wed (A) 26/12/1911, V West Ham (A)

19/10/1968 and v Watford (A) 25/9/1982 (All Div 1)

FA Cup: 27/1/1934, 2-7, v Aston Villa (A)

League Cup: 31/10/1990, 0-6, v Derby County (A)

Age Records:

Oldest Player: Pop Robson, 38 years and 182 days.

Youngest Player: Derek Forster, 15 years 184 days.

Picture Gallery

Peter Reid

Charlie Parker, a centre half with more than 250 appearances during the 1920s.

Jim Montgomery

An Agreement made the _12th._ day of

April 19 _21_ between _Robt H. Kyle._ of _Sunderland_ in the County of _Durham._ the Secretary of and acting pursuant to Resolution and Authority for and on behalf of the _Sunderland. F._ Club — of _Sunderland_ in the County of _Durham._ (hereinafter referred to as the Club) of the one part and _John Johnston._ of _Sunderland_ in the County of — _Durham_ Professional Football Player (hereinafter referred to as the Player) of the other part **Whereby** it is agreed as follows :—

1. The Player hereby agrees to play in an efficient manner and to the best of his ability for the Club.

2. The Player shall attend the Club's ground or any other place decided upon by the Club for the purposes of or in connection with his training as a Player pursuant to the instructions of the Secretary, Manager or Trainer of the Club or of such other person or persons as the Club may appoint.

3. The Player shall do everything necessary to get and keep himself in the best possible condition so as to render the most efficient service to the Club and will carry out all the training and other instructions of the Club through its representative officials.

4. The Player shall observe and be subject to all the Rules, Regulations and Bye-laws of the Football Association, the Football League, the Southern League, the Inter-League Board, the English League Board, the Anglo-Irish League Board and any other Association, League or Combination of which the Club shall be a member. And this Agreement shall be subject to any action which shall be taken by the Football Association under Rule 26 of their Rules for the suspension or termination of the Football Season, and if any such suspension or termination shall be decided upon the payment of wages provided for in Clause 8 shall likewise be suspended or terminated as the case may be.

Contract of John Johnston, five appearances in the early 1920s.

7. In consideration of the observance by the said Player of the terms provisions and conditions of this Agreement, the said _Robt H. Kyle._ on behalf of the Club hereby agrees that the said Club shall pay to the said Player the sum of £ _6 – 0 – 0_ per week, from _May 9th 1921_ to _May 6th 1922._

8. This Agreement shall cease and determine on _May 6th 1922._ unless the same shall have been previously determined in accordance with the provisions hereinbefore set forth.

Fill in any other provisions required.

and £7 – 0 – 0 per week from Jan 1st 1922 to May 6th 1922. if playing in the first team.

As Witness the hands of the said parties the day and year first aforesaid

Signed by the said _Robt. H. Kyle._

and _John Johnston._

Robt H. Kyle

In the presence of

(SIGNATURE) _W. Williams_

(OCCUPATION) _Trainer_

(ADDRESS) _Sunderland_

John Johnston

FORM OF NOTICE TO TERMINATE AGREEMENT.

I the undersigned as Secretary for and on behalf of the.. Club do hereby.................give you.................................days' notice of the intention of the said Club to terminate the agreement of service dated the.....................................day of ....192 entered into between you and the Club on the following ground (or grounds).

And further take notice that you have a right of appeal to the Management Committee of the Football League but such appeal must be made within seven days of the receipt of this Notice. Such appeal will be heard within ten days of the receipt of the notice of appeal from you. If you are dissatisfied with the decision of the Management Committee you have a further right of appeal to the Appeals Committee of the League appointed for that purpose by the Football Association but such further appeal must be made by you within seven days of the receipt of the intimation of the decision of the Management Committee and must be accompanied by a deposit of £5. The Appeals Committee will hear such appeal within ten days of the receipt of the notice of appeal.

All notices of appeal must be in writing and addressed to Mr. T. CHARNLEY, Castle Chambers, Market Place, Preston.

Raich Carter

Ian Porterfield scores the goal in the 1-0 FA Cup Final victory over Leeds in 1973 at Wembley.

Kevin Ball, captain of the new First Division Championship winning sides of 1996 and 1999.